WITHDRAWN

D0310193

DARTMOOR NATIONAL PARK

ORDNANCE SURVEY 2½ INCH MAP
SHEET NUMBERS

The Ordnance Survey One-Inch Tourist Map
of Dartmoor covers all the Park

DARTMOOR

★

NATIONAL PARK GUIDE No. I

ISSUED FOR THE
NATIONAL PARKS COMMISSION

REISSUED FOR THE
COUNTRYSIDE COMMISSION 1968

LONDON
HER MAJESTY'S STATIONERY OFFICE
1957

Crown copyright reserved

First published 1957
Fifth impression 1972
(with amendments)

*This guide-book was prepared by the
Dartmoor National Park Committee under
the editorship of Professor W. G. Hoskins,
President of the
Dartmoor Preservation Association*

SBN 11 700478 2

PREFACE

THE designation of Dartmoor as a National Park marked it out as one of Britain's finest landscape areas, a national asset whose unique and characteristic natural beauty must be protected from spoliation and preserved for the enjoyment of the nation.

The Dartmoor National Park Committee are to be congratulated, not only on having prepared this excellent book, but also on being the first Park Planning Authority to provide an official guide-book for a National Park. The National Parks Commission are glad to have had the opportunity of being associated with them in its production.

It has often seemed that too few of those who visit Dartmoor are aware that it is one of our best scenic areas and that too few seek the inspiration and relaxation which are to be found in its fine wooded valleys, its wide upland landscape, its relics from man's remote past and its many other attractions for rider and walker alike.

This guide-book will do great service in making known to those who visit Dartmoor its varied attractions and its outstanding merit as a holiday area.

I warmly commend this guide to all who seek to know the Moor.

LORD STRANG

Chairman of the National Parks Commission 1954-66

CONTENTS

The cover drawing is of the Dewerstone Rock at the meeting of the Meavy and the Plym and is taken from the frontispiece of *Amid Devonia's Alps* by William Crossing.

ACKNOWLEDGMENTS

We wish to acknowledge the kindness of the executors of the will of the late Mr. R. H. Worth for allowing us to reproduce plates 15, 19, 25 and Fig. 2. We are also indebted to the Council of the Prehistoric Society for permission to reproduce Fig. 1, and to Lady Sayer for allowing us to reproduce her line drawing at Fig. 3.

Photographs for plates 16 and 17 were contributed by Hope Bagenal, F.R.I.B.A.; for plates 1, 3, 4, 9, 18, 20, 21 and 23 by A. V. Bibbings; for plate 10 by Chapman & Sons, Dawlish; for plate 11 by Aubrey L. Parminter; for plate 24 by Lady Sayer; for plates 2, 5, 6, 7, 8, 12, 13 and 22 by E. H. Ware, and plate 14 by D. P. Wilson, to whom grateful thanks are due.

ILLUSTRATIONS

LINE DRAWINGS (FIGURES)

MAPS

INTRODUCTION

BY SIR HENRY SLESSER

Formerly Chairman of the Dartmoor National Park Committee

I HAVE been asked, as Chairman of the Dartmoor National Park Committee, to write a few words by way of introduction to this book. This I cannot do more usefully than by appealing to you, the reader, to co-operate with us in preserving the beauty and perfection of this natural magnificence, as I am sure you will.

First and foremost, we feel that the scattering of litter of every kind, paper, cardboard, bottles or whatever it may be, though not a permanent injury perhaps, does sadly destroy the feeling of undisturbed peace and grandeur which is so characteristic of Dartmoor unblemished. Particularly can rubbish be an inescapable eyesore where people congregate in so-called 'beauty spots'—as if all the Moor were not beautiful! Glass, especially, is very dangerous, to both animals and riders, and is none the better for being concealed in bushes of gorse and the like which are often exposed in the winter.

Secondly, may I mention the danger of fires. A large area of the Moor is planted with National Forests, and the loss to the nation if these burn is very great. Also it is most unfortunate if the gorse and heather are burned, save under precaution by experienced farmers at proper times: the process known as swaling. A wide tract of Moor may be ruined for the time by exposing a large blackened mass, the result, too often, of the careless discarding of lighted cigarettes or matches or careless kindling of twigs for a picnic. Animals also may be put in danger if the fire spreads, and no one would wish this.

Thirdly, there are many farms in and around the Moor and most of the farmers are now raising attested herds of cattle, so that it is vital that there shall be no promiscuous straying. Therefore, if you are passing through a farm or its fields and have occasion to open a gate, do please see that it is carefully closed behind you.

Antiquities need care. Such things as standing stones, barrows, cairns, hut circles, medieval crosses, or any of the monuments you will see on the Moor—an ill-advised action can in five minutes disturb or obliterate evidence which has survived a thousand years or more.

Lastly, if you are a motorist, it will be borne in on you that most of our roads leading to the Moor itself are very winding and, in many places, very narrow. Careful driving is essential—the natives know it—but I must admit, as Chairman of a local bench, that the number of prosecutions for careless and dangerous driving greatly increases when the summer season begins. A further danger arises from the feeding of ponies on the road. Harmless though this appears to be, it makes the animals careless of traffic and a serious danger to themselves and to motorists. By-laws now operate making it illegal to feed ponies on a road.

I am aware that these words are of a cautionary kind. We realize that there are many who do, in fact, appreciate that the Park is an invaluable national possession. But the fact is that there are still people who, either through ignorance or from indifference, have failed to give us that mutual assistance without which our work as guardians of the Park can be so easily set at nought.

We, in our turn, try to do everything possible to preserve the Moor. We seek to prevent the erection of unsuitable or unsightly buildings, and this obligation extends to the Moor, and for this purpose the National Parks Commission and the Minister responsible agreed to the fixing of the Park boundary far beyond the actual moorland area itself—in any case much of the Park's greatest beauty lies in the wooded and watered valleys leading up to the Moor itself.

In accordance with our objectives, and with the co-operation of Parish and District Councils, we have already caused many unsightly objects—dumps of old wire, old disused huts of galvanized iron and the like—some left from the war or military exercises, to be removed. We are still tackling the problems of ugly and inappropriate advertisements, of the preservation of ancient monuments and buildings, and the preservation of villages and hamlets within our area from commercial vulgarization, and generally anything which menaces or threatens to menace the age-long solitude and integrity of the Moor: there are not many such heritages in England.

The ten National Parks which have been constituted in England and Wales owe their origin to the recommendations made in the Dower Report of 1945 and in the Hobhouse Report of 1947 presented to Parliament by the then Minister of Town and Country Planning. After close examination many of their suggestions were embodied in a Statute, the National Parks and Access to the Countryside Act, 1949.

It was under this Act that the Dartmoor National Park was designated in 1951 and a special standing committee of the Devon County Council were subsequently set up to carry out the objects of the Act within the National Park. The primary purpose of the committee, as stated in the Act, acting in consultation with the Countryside Commission, is 'to preserve the natural beauty of the district and give opportunities for open-air recreation'. We are required, among other matters, to formulate proposals as to the action to be taken to achieve the objects of the National Park, in particular to deal with accommodation, camping sites, parking places and access to the 'open country'. The problem of access is not a difficult matter in this instance since, by long-standing custom, persons may wander at will over Dartmoor's open country and it has not, up to the time of writing, been considered necessary or advisable by the committee to seek Access Agreements with the owners concerned.*

The Dartmoor Committee have also, for their own guidance, already laid down principles as to the sanction of camping sites, the encouragement of building in keeping with the local tradition, the removal of disfigurements—this activity being complicated by the duty to provide compensation in some cases—and many other matters, such as claims for afforestation and the thinning or destruction of woodlands, the demand by public authorities—military and other—for land use or electric overhead wires and by commercial interests seeking to win minerals or erect factories and plant and, generally, to reconcile utilitarian considerations with the maintenance of the Moor in its unspoiled state. The rights and customs of farmers, owners of land, and commoners, have also to be considered.

The Dartmoor National Park Committee meet normally once a month and have had to appoint many sub-committees to deal with such matters as the inspection of prospective building sites, menaced woodlands, proposed reservoirs and other planning problems affecting the Moor and its environs. They number eighteen members, twelve directly appointed annually by the Devon County Council and six nominated by the Secretary of State for the Environment for consideration by the council. From time to time they receive advice from the Countryside Commission. Within the limits of their opportunity and resources, the committee are doing what they can to maintain the Park in its state of 'outstanding natural beauty', to quote the words of the Statute constituting the National Park.

It is for this purpose that Parliament has invested us, by delegation from the Devon County Council, with considerable powers under the Planning and National Parks Acts. We have also the right under county by-laws to prosecute for the scattering of litter, feeding of animals, or unlawful lighting of fires, but our aim, ever since we were legally established, has been rather to seek to accomplish our task and fulfil our duties by mutual agreement and discussion. In this we have succeeded with most of the local residents; and that is why we are appealing to you for full co-operation to hand down the Moor to posterity, even more free from the blemishes which have been imposed from time to time upon it than it was when we took over the proud responsibility of being its statutory custodians.

* Since this was written, two such access agreements have in fact been concluded, one at Fingle Bridge and the other at Roborough Down.

I

The Geology, Physiography and Climate of Dartmoor

BY DR. ALFRED SHORTER

Formerly Montefiore Reader in Geography, University of Exeter

GEOLOGY

DARTMOOR is one of the five granite masses or 'bosses' which form the core of much of South-West England. In structure and scenery it has certain close affinities with Bodmin Moor and the other granite moors of Cornwall, but it is much the largest and the highest of the bosses. It dominates much of Devon, and from it water flows to almost all the Devonshire rivers west of the Exe.

These granite masses represent the stumps of a mountain system which was formed millions of years ago. With the upheaval of this system came the intrusion of granite into the folds of the mountains, and this molten material was continuously pushed up under the stratified rocks on the earth's surface. After intrusion, the granite cooled, crystallized and hardened, and the surface sedimentary rocks have gradually been worn off, so that the granite has long been exposed to weathering.

The rocks surrounding the Dartmoor boss were mainly shales, grits, cherts and limestones. These rocks were metamorphosed (baked and hardened) by heat from the molten material, the zone of alteration around the granite core being called a 'metamorphic aureole'. Farther away from the granite, the sedimentaries which were altered, warped and distorted by the folding and intrusion gradually pass into unchanged rocks.

Within the granite and the aureole, vapours associated with the igneous activity were responsible for the formation of minerals such as the ores of tin, copper, lead, silver, iron, manganese and arsenic. Fissures in the rock were filled in by metallic compounds; in this way were formed the lodes, which many millions of years later were found, traced and worked by miners. Vapours from within also affected the granite to produce china clay by a process called kaolinization, which involved a chemical change of the felspar crystals of the granite. The sands, lignite and clays of the infilled Bovey Basin (around the lower Bovey and Teign rivers) were deposited much later by fresh-water torrents coming down from the granite area.

Much of the Dartmoor granite is coarse-grained, containing large crystals of porphyritic felspar. The other chief constituents of the granite are quartz, black mica (biotite), tourmaline and white mica (muscovite), which have different degrees of resistance to attack. The sparkling fragments of insoluble quartz and mica can readily be distinguished in the spoil-heaps where the china clay has been worked in Cornwall and on southern Dartmoor. The granite has weathered into different blocks, surfaces and soils because of the various ways in which it was jointed and the different rates at which its materials have broken down. The position, aspect and slope of the rock also played an important part. Although proverbially hard, the granite has in many places become quite rotten, weathering into a subsoil called 'growan'. Much of the soil is peat of various thicknesses, but there are also light-weight gravelly soils. Digging can thus be done at many places on the Moor, using ordinary tools and no great effort.

Granite forms the greater part of the National Park area, but there are other rocks to be seen within and around the boundary of the Park, including igneous, metamorphics and sedimentaries. To the west of Dartmoor stands Brentor (1,130 feet), a steep-sided mass of lava. Other evidence of igneous activity is seen on the eastern side, in the Teign valley and the hills around, where igneous rocks have long been quarried, and, where suitable, used as building stones. Perhaps the most distinctive and attractive of all the volcanic building stones is the green stone from the Hurdwick quarries (now disused) which may be seen extensively in Tavistock and the surrounding district.

PHYSIOGRAPHY

Dartmoor is not a mountainous region, but a broad, rolling upland of an average elevation of 1,200 feet (Plate 4). It is often described as essentially a table-land or plateau, but it has greater diversity of surface features than these words suggest (Plate 1). There is a marked contrast between the rolling granite hills and the level tracts which occur here and there around the Moor, and considerable diversity in successive stretches of the valleys in the granite country and the gorges in and around the Park area.

Good examples of the generally rounded form of the granite hills are to be seen from the approaches to the Moor, for instance Cosdon (Cawsand), seen from the Exeter–Okehampton road. The relatively easy rotting of the granite due to weathering largely accounts for the comparatively gentle slopes, the rolling type of country, and the rather wide, shallow valleys. Steep valley sides are rare, because rotted granite will not stand in such slopes. Where solid granite crosses a valley the sides may be locally steeper, even gorge-like, as in Tavy Cleave.

Differences in general height suggest a division of the granite country into three regions—the northern, southern and eastern areas; the line dividing the first two approximates to the Moretonhampstead–Prince-town road. The northern part of the granite core rises to the highest points on the Moor, in the masses of High Willhays (2,038 feet) and Yes Tor (2,030 feet). In the southern part only a few hills, for example Hamel Down and Ryder's Hill, rise to over 1,600 feet. The third and much smaller area lies east of a line drawn through Chagford and at right-angles to the above-mentioned road. Its highest parts are between 900 and 1,200 feet above sea level.

Of all the rivers which rise in the high northern area, only two—the Taw and the Okement (via the Torridge)—flow to the north coast of Devon. The Dart and its tributaries drain a large part of the Moor, but many other rivers which rise in different parts of Dartmoor also flow in a generally southerly direction; the Avon, Erme, Yealm and Plym are examples. During periods when there is continuously heavy rain many small runnels appear on the saturated ground and there is a spectacular surface run-off; in time of flood the rivers rise and fall very rapidly. It is true that during heavy rain the peat takes up plenty of water, but when saturated it functions like an impermeable rock and any further rain runs off its surface. Not all the water absorbed by the peat eventually drains away to the rivers; much of it merely dries out. Fortunately water which penetrates to the thick layer of growan (see page 2) is there stored; it moves slowly through the rotted granite to feed the streams after the supplies from the surface run-off have dwindled and disappeared, and is released comparatively gently as from a sponge.

On the granite the upper stretches of the rivers are fairly placid, except in flood, but they have variety. A stretch of gentle flow may be broken by many pools, low shelves of rock across the river bed, small cascades and boulders (Plate 6). There are no natural lakes, but where the gradient lessens there are sometimes broad flats, of which Taw Marsh is an example. Another feature of some of the Dartmoor valleys is the waste heaps left by the tin-streamers where they followed and worked over the valley bottoms. The deep gashes and gullies which were made by tin-workers on the sides of some of the valleys must not be mistaken for the results of natural erosion. Good examples of former tin-works are to be seen about half a mile west of Grimspound, and at Birch Tor and Vitifer (Plate 13) near Warren House Inn.

Among the distinctive features of the Dartmoor landscape is the 'tor', which is usually a mass of unrotted granite that has been left as a cap on a hill above the general level of the table-land. The tors differ greatly in size and appearance. Blackingstone Rock (near Moretonhampstead) is a dome-shaped mass, while Haytor (near Widecombe) is remarkable for its humps. Staple Tor (near Merrivale) consists of a series of steeple-like piles of blocks, while Bowerman's Nose (near Manaton) is a single pile or stack. In the course of weathering, many of the upper and outer blocks of the tors have been rounded into comparatively soft outlines (Plate 2), but nevertheless there are some remarkably odd shapes which emphasize the individuality of the tors, some of which are thought to bear a resemblance to human beings or animals. Many of the tors show structural weaknesses which resulted from the cooling and contraction of the granite. Examples are to be seen in the false or pseudo-bedding (the appearance of stratification in the rock) which may be set close or wide, and may run horizontally or parallel with the ground. There are also vertical and inclined joints, which have facilitated splitting and weathering. The tops of the tors occasionally bear the evidence of atmospheric attack in the shape of the 'rock basins' incised in the surface, where the successive actions of frost, thaw, moisture and wind have gradually removed small flakes of granite and have thus eaten out hollows. These basins vary considerably in size up to about three feet in the maximum cross-measurement.

The 'clitters' or 'clatters' are another distinctive feature of the granite country. A typical clitter consists of tumbled granitic debris, including many large fragments, strewn along or down a slope below a tor. On some slopes there is an open scatter of rocks, but in other clitters the blocks are pressed so closely that there is little room for soil or vegetation between them. Good examples are to be seen on Hen Tor (near Shaugh Prior), where the slopes are in places densely packed with stones. Such clitters are the remains of material which in past periods of very cold climate moved outwards and downwards from the tors, sliding and creeping on ice and snow. The finer elements in this material have long since been removed by the action of water and wind, but the larger blocks remain.

It has sometimes been argued that certain of the surface features of Dartmoor are due to glaciation, but this view is not generally accepted. During the Ice Ages, Dartmoor must have been covered by snow and ice for long periods, but not by a continuous thick ice sheet or by glaciers. There is no evidence here that can really be attributed to the scouring action of ice or the deposition of moraines.

The erosion of the rocks on the margins of Dartmoor—the metamorphics and the shales and other sedimentaries—has produced generally steeper slopes than are seen on the granite. The valley sides do not open out by weathering as easily as they do on granite, and steep slopes will stand more readily on the metamorphics. The rivers, too, have a different character. While some of the valleys on the outer granite area are certainly fairly deep-cut and are much broken by boulders, cascades or waterfalls, as in Lustleigh Cleave, Tavy Cleave or at Becka Falls (near Manaton), others suddenly deepen in or near the zone where they emerge from the granite. The West Okement and the Teign, for example, there enter deep narrow ravines (Plate 3). The incision of the streams is accounted for by an uplift of the land which occurred comparatively recently in geological time, whereby the waters have cut deeply into the sedimentary rocks and the metamorphics. On the western fringe of Dartmoor the River Lyd has cut a spectacular course in such rocks. Some four miles below its source it plunges into a deep chasm, where excellent examples of smooth-rounded potholes can be seen at various levels on the sides and bottom, then into a wider section through the shales, with a beautiful tributary waterfall (locally known as The White Lady) coming in on the left side.

CLIMATE

The prevalent westerly winds, nearness to the sea, and height give Dartmoor much rain, mist and hill fog. Few statistics are available about the climate of the high, remote northern areas; the western and southern parts have a wet or moderately wet climate, and the eastern area is appreciably drier. The heaviest rainfalls occur probably on the windward side of the first western hills which rise to about 1,400 feet and meet the south-west winds. The figures for the period 1951–70 show that at Princetown the mean annual rainfall was 86 inches, and that some rain fell on 218 days in the year. The amount measured on many of these days was, however, small and was due to light rain or showers. This recording station, at a height of 1,359 feet, is certainly in one of the wettest areas where records are kept on the Moor, and it should not, of course, be taken as typical of the whole of the National Park area. Over the same period, however, nearly 80 inches of rain a year was recorded at the Cowsic valley station which is also on western Dartmoor, at 1,323 feet. Only a slightly lower mean annual rainfall was recorded at White Ridge, which lies further east but at a height of 1,650 feet. The stations on the eastern margins show a lower mean figure; Laployd (at a height of 1,041 feet) had over 48 inches, but much of the lower part of the eastern area probably had appreciably less.

Normally, much of the rain on Dartmoor falls in the late autumn and early winter; November and December are often particularly wet. In 1929, 29·36 inches fell at Princetown in November, followed by 19·58 inches in December. 24·61 inches fell in December 1934. There have also been very heavy individual falls in 24 hours, for examples on 23 November 1946 (6·83 inches at Princetown, H.M. Prison), and on 28 July 1969 (5·69 inches at North Hessary Tor).

Fog may be rather frequent and sometimes develops rapidly. Much of it consists of low clouds which result from the rise of damp air over the western edge of the Moor. There are days in the summer when the warmth and humidity may give an oppressive feeling, but thunderstorms are not frequent.

Above about 1,000 feet snow falls on some twenty-five days in the year; it lies for twenty days or more on the higher parts, and probably for thirty or more on the highest. Some of the great general snowstorms on the Moor have been accompanied by high winds, resulting in much drifting of snow over and off Dartmoor. Such storms have been followed by the isolation of many settlements by deep snow; but more usually the snowfall is short-lived and irregular.

Average temperatures are of course below those of much of Devon. The mean daily maximum for the year at Princetown is between four and five degrees Fahrenheit lower than that at Torquay.

These climatic statistics and generalizations conceal the varied and often attractive weather which one may experience even in a short stay on Dartmoor. To those who have known the Moor at all seasons there come memories of many days spent in soft air and warm sunshine, of sharp but short-lived storms, of boisterous, invigorating winds, and of the exhilaration felt after snow; memories, too, of the clarity and purity of the atmosphere after rain, and of rapid variations in light and shade and in the type and density of cloud. After a drought (as in late summer 1959 and again in spring 1960) much of the ground can be quite hard and dry; and the open moor on a fine summer's day can be very hot through the entire absence of shade. Visitors should be prepared for such perhaps unexpected aspects of the climate.

BIBLIOGRAPHY

Memoirs of the Geological Survey, England and Wales, Explanation of Sheet 338, The Geology of Dartmoor, 1912. Essential to an understanding of the detail of the geology of the National Park area.

PERKINS, J. W. *Geology Explained: Dartmoor and the Tamar Valley.* David & Charles. 1972.

SHORTER, A. H., RAVENHILL, W. L. D., and GREGORY, K. J. *South-West England.* 1968. Includes references to many aspects of the physiography and topography of Dartmoor.

SIMMONDS, I. G. (ed.). *Dartmoor Essays.* 1964. Published by the Devonshire Association. Contains essays on the geology and geomorphology of the Moor.

WORTH, R. H. *Dartmoor.* 1953. New edition published by David & Charles (1967). Chapter on The Physical Geography of Dartmoor. A detailed and well-illustrated survey, based on a study of Dartmoor at first hand over many years.

Climatic statistics for the stations mentioned in this chapter and for various other places on and around Dartmoor are given annually in the *Transactions of the Devonshire Association.*

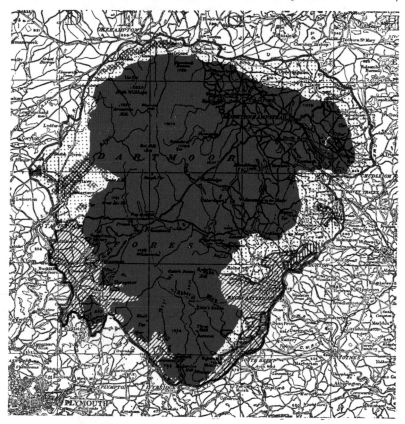

MAP 2. The geology of the Dartmoor National Park

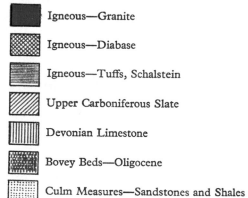

Igneous—Granite

Igneous—Diabase

Igneous—Tuffs, Schalstein

Upper Carboniferous Slate

Devonian Limestone

Bovey Beds—Oligocene

Culm Measures—Sandstones and Shales

2

The Natural History of Dartmoor

BY L. A. HARVEY

Formerly Professor of Zoology, University of Exeter

THE area embraced by the Dartmoor National Park extends beyond the borders of the ancient Forest of Dartmoor and its Commons and includes a fringe of 'in-country'. This is entirely logical, for this marginal region belongs both by its geological history and by its topographical structure to Dartmoor rather than to the lowlands. The biological conditions of this 'in-country' are, however, transitional in character, introducing new elements into the flora and fauna which belong to a pastoral countryside rather than to the moors.

The Moor proper overlies the granite core of the region. It is all situated at a relatively high altitude, and lies close to the western seaboard of Britain. As a consequence, temperatures are low, rainfall high, and the normal processes of decay which break down the dead remains of plants and animals into humus are not completed, stopping short with the production of an acid peat soil. Such conditions combine to influence both flora and fauna, mostly by limitation and exclusion. Apart from lichens and mosses, there are comparatively few plants which are adapted to survive and flourish under these conditions, and on the higher, wetter centre of Dartmoor we find two great areas of blanket bog. The northern bog is the larger, filling the highland from Okehampton, to the north, to within about a mile of the Moretonhampstead-Princetown road between Two Bridges and Postbridge. The southern bog is centred on the watershed from which rise the Rivers Avon, Erme and Plym. These bogs are immensely important to the Moor, as indeed to all Devon, as the source of its rivers; but they present, to most minds, a bleak and forbidding aspect. Nowadays, for reasons not understood, there is little active peat formation. Indeed, what evidence there is suggests its regression. Hence, over this rolling upland there is spread a carpet of olive, brown and purple, broken only by the grey rocks of the upstanding tors, the richer browns of the exposed peat hags, and here and there by the shine of water and of the multitudinous tassels of the bog cottons (Plate 7). The vegetation, like that of a tundra, is dominated by mosses and lichens, purple moor grass (*Molinia coerulea*), the two bog cottons, *Eriophorum angustifolium* and *Eriophorum vaginatum*, in the wetter places, and many other smaller sedges. The heathers are thinly scattered, and of them the cross-leaved heath, *Erica tetralix*, is the most

8

PLATE 1. Haytor from Hound Tor

PLATE 2. Granite formation at Hound Tor

PLATE 3. General view of the Teign valley

PLATE 4. The edge of Dartmoor: West Webburn valley with Hamel Down beyond

frequent. The poor pasturage, and the soft going, deter most of the larger animals. Few ponies or cattle are to be found here, and even sheep are scanty. Nor are there many smaller animals, the mammals and birds being for the most part confined to wide-ranging species which can voyage into and across the bogs from the more hospitable surrounding country. The few breeding birds to be found include curlew, common sandpiper, lapwing, and possibly merlin.

Unattractive as this picture of the blanket bogs may be they can be very rewarding. A walk across the northern bog from Two Bridges, via Fur Tor and Cut Hill, to Cranmere Pool presents many panoramic views, and one never knows what may turn up in the bog carpet. Moreover, there is great satisfaction to be had in the achievement of an arduous journey across the quavering peat hags on the top. Further, it can be the quietest of places for those who love solitude, with only the occasional bark of a raven, or the golden bubbling of a curlew to break the silence.

Over the ring of moorlands surrounding these bogs, although mosses and lichens are still very numerous, they are far less evident, being canopied over by the now much more vigorous flowering plants. Certain of these species may be so dominant on a hillside as to give their name to the moor. Thus, heather moor, whortleberry moor and grass moor may occur. It is the heather moors which are associated in most people's minds with Dartmoor, and they cover vast stretches. The dominant species is the true heather or ling, *Calluna vulgaris*; but bell heather, *Erica cinerea*, although less abundant, is nevertheless an integral part of the plant carpet, particularly along roadside banks, or where the ground is scarred by old tin-workings. The other heather, cross-leaved heath, comes into prominence in the wetter, boggy regions. Our remaining two English heathers, Cornish heath, *Erica vagans*, and Dorset heath, *Erica ciliaris*, cannot be regarded as Dartmoor plants. Cornish heath was, we know, introduced near Lydford where I believe it still grows, although I have never visited this colony. The origin of the small, but vigorously growing stand of Dorset heath near Headland Warren is quite unknown. The plant flourishes there, having survived fire and the planting operations of the Forestry Commission. The colony having been inadvertently enclosed within a plantation, the Commission have, with commendable solicitude, left a small area about it unplanted with trees in order to ensure its preservation.

The heather and grass moors provide the main pasturage for the large head of stock which Dartmoor carries, and as a consequence they have undergone a marked transformation from their original, wild, condition. Old, well-matured heather is very difficult to find on Dartmoor. When found it makes a tall straggly bush, some two feet or more high, with long twisting tough woody stems each bearing a thin canopy

B

of leaves and blooms. Such plants make very poor pasture, besides encumbering the ground with a deep wiry cover, and all heather moors on which stock are kept are managed by periodic burning, the local name for this procedure being 'swaling'. This, if properly controlled, kills the woody stems without damaging the roots, and from the latter a new luxuriant growth of green, succulent shoots rapidly springs. In two or three years a thick leafy carpet covers the ground, flowering richly in late summer, and is a very beautiful sight. Unfortunately, swaling on Dartmoor has got out of hand in many places, and, in particular, youths and young children burn indiscriminately, and with little concern for the season of the year. In consequence, the heather's vitality is sapped, while bracken is favoured. The latter has spread much too widely during recent years.

Here is not the place to discuss the domestic animals of the Moor, but a word or two should be said about the ponies. These sturdy little horses constitute a characteristic feature of the moorland scene, and it is surprising that so little is known about them. There is, however, a remarkable early reference to them in the will of the Saxon bishop Aelfwold of Crediton (997–1012) who left 'to the atheling forty mancuses of gold and the wild horses on the land at Ashburton'. The Ashburton estate stretched well into the Moor and there can be little doubt that this reference to 'wild horses' relates to the ancestors of the present animals. There is no evidence of wild horses having survived in Britain up to the time when man came on the scene, unless indeed the ponies of Exmoor are, as has been postulated, such relicts. Moreover, the falling mane of the Dartmoor pony contrasts sharply with the stiff, erect mane of such extant wild horses as Przewalsky's and the tarpan. It appears that neither Bronze Age nor Iron Age man on Dartmoor used horses extensively, and it therefore seems probable that it was at some time during the Dark Ages that animals turned out on the Moor went feral, so becoming the ancestors of the Dartmoors we see today. The Minister's Accounts of the Earldom of Cornwall for 1296–7 may be significant in this context, referring as they do to the fee of twopence a head for the pasturing of 487 horses throughout the year. Since that time the stock has become moulded by natural selection into a small, sturdy yet slender animal, of quite variable colour, but very hardy and active. The ponies of today are all too rarely typical of the breed, which has been diluted time and again by intercrossing with other types. Although left to run wild over the Moor throughout the year—and incidentally, until the installation of cattle grids across all approach roads, sometimes becoming a nuisance by invading the gardens of moorland villages during spells of hard weather— all the animals have owners, and annual pony drifts are held in the autumn, at which the ponies are rounded up, and the foals of the year branded with their owners' marks. Many are sold, going from Dartmoor, some to the pits, some to be broken as children's mounts, and some to the Continental meat markets. When grazing on the Moor the animals are not usually approachable, but, particularly at some beauty spots where cars and coaches park, some of the ponies have learned to come and beg for food, a practice which has its dangers for the animals which tend to become somewhat indifferent to the approach of cars, and also for those who feed them, since they are liable to be bitten or kicked if the animal should be startled. Indeed, within the last few years it has been found necessary to forbid their being fed by the public and notices to this effect are now displayed at all critical sites.

The word 'warren' incorporated into many Dartmoor place-names— Headland, Ditsworthy, Trowlesworthy Warren for instance—commemorates the introduction of another feral mammal, the rabbit. The Normans probably introduced this animal into England for sporting purposes, creating the colonies or warrens, each with a warrener in charge. From here, the rabbits, well able to look after themselves, spread widely, and it is only since the introduction of myxomatosis that they have met a serious check. Of our other mammals perhaps the most notable on Dartmoor, being relatively easy to find, is the fox, which is abundant in many places and frequently lies out in thick bracken or heather, from which it may be flushed by the walker. Badger and otter are also there, but being much more nocturnal in habits, are only to be found by those prepared to take some little trouble. Every year a few red deer move across from Exmoor, but they are never allowed to establish themselves. The only representatives of the woodland deer are the Japanese sikas which have been introduced in the neighbourhood of Moretonhampstead where they are now feral.

It is impossible to walk over these moors without encountering bogs, which present themselves in various conditions and sizes, from the 'featherbeds', brilliant green basins only a yard or so across filled with sphagnum, to the extensive marshes which may fill a whole valley floor, particularly where it shallows off at the level of an old shoreline. Few of these bogs are dangerous, although many present considerable obstacles on the way. For my own part I get the greatest enjoyment from wading about in the often knee-deep cushion of springy peat and sphagnum, and seeking the delicately brilliant plants which flourish in them. This is by far the best way to find some of Dartmoor's loveliest flowers: the sundews, both round-leaved and intermediate, an infinite variety of sedges, and those tiny charmers, bog pimpernel, bog campanula, lesser skullcap and pale butterwort. The latter plant replaces the common butterwort in western Britain, being a representative of a small

relict flora known as Lusitanian, which survived the Glacial Period along
our southern and western coasts and commemorates an earlier affinity
with Portugal and Spain. Here too may be found lousewort, bog
asphodel, beautiful in its golden yellow starlike flowers as also in the
rusty red of its seed spikes, and the shyly blooming marsh St. John's
Wort, the soft hairy leaves of which seem always bedewed with a mist of
silvery water droplets.

The small animal life of the moors calls for brief mention. The
characteristic birds, to list only the more outstanding, are the wide-
ranging buzzard (Plate 8), the raven, carrion crow, and kestrel, together
with skylark and meadow pipit nesting among the tussocks of grass and
heather; and in summer, wheatears about the boulders of the stone walls
and antiquities, the tors and the clitters; stonechat and whinchat among
the gorse, dipper and grey wagtail along the watercourses, and a few
small colonies of ring ouzels in the deeper valleys. Of reptiles, both the
common lizard and adder are frequent. The former often betrays itself
by its swift sinuous running among the heather, into the depths of
which it disappears when disturbed. Although adders are common
enough, particularly on rocky ground, they are not often seen, and they
need cause even the most timid little concern. Far from being aggressive,
they are extremely sensitive to vibration, and have usually vanished long
before the walker has approached.

Shelled snails are uncommon on these lime-free soils, but slugs are
more frequent, the handsome glistening black slug, *Arion ater*, being
ubiquitous along the grassy sheep tracks. Only a few insects can be
selected for mention. Dragonflies can be very abundant in this wet area,
notable among them being *Cordulegaster boltonii*, in vivid black and
yellow, which breeds in the streams, and the pale blue *Orthetrum
coerulescens* of the bog pools. The emperor moth may be seen flying
rapidly in sunshine over the heather during early summer, and its beautiful green and black banded caterpillar, the narrow black bands picked
out with orange warts, may be searched for in the heather throughout
the year. But, although so large and apparently conspicuous, it is
remarkably well concealed in the densely speckled fronds of its habitat;
the chocolate and gold banded larva of the fox moth is much more frequently found. In certain of the marshier valleys, where its food plant,
devil's bit scabious, is abundant, the marsh fritillary occurs, and a small
colony of the now all too rare large blue butterfly exists in a locality the
whereabouts of which cannot be disclosed. In addition to the honey bees,
hives of which are brought to Dartmoor for the heather honey season,
there are numerous solitary and humble bees, the most outstanding of
which is *Bombus lapponicus*, a species restricted to such high moorlands.
Many flies are to be found, and the dipterist will be interested in the

manner in which species of this group appear to be attracted in fine summer weather to the tops of the tors. This phenomenon, which is not confined to the Diptera, has been observed recently by local entomologists, but its causes, and indeed its full extent, have yet to be determined.

The woodlands in the National Park include many of its most lovely and interesting places. The visitor must not be misled by the ancient name, the Forest of Dartmoor, into the belief that these high hills were once entirely tree-covered. It is only comparatively recently that the word 'forest' has come to be restricted to wooded land. Its original meaning denoted a tract of land reserved, usually by the king, in its wild condition for hunting and subject to special forest laws, and the forest of Dartmoor was such a reserve. There is no evidence that Dartmoor was forested during historic times, and the climate of the uplands today may be too severe for hardwoods, although these may grow in the valleys. Until the peat deposits of the Moor have been analysed we must remain largely ignorant of past floras, but occasional finds of stumps and logs preserved in the peat have indicated that oak, birch and hazel were formerly more widespread than they are now. It is possible that the tinners of the Middle Ages were responsible for much disafforestation in the search for fuel for their smelting-houses. Even so it seems probable that such woods as may have existed at that time only crept higher up the valleys and did not extend over the hill-tops.

The surviving woods include the three ancient upland copses, Wistman's Wood, Black Tor Beare and Piles Copse; a considerable extent of plantations, for the most part of conifers, some dating back to the early years of the century, such as Brimpts and Tor Royal, and others more modern, under the control of the Forestry Commission; and finally the indigenous oakwoods of the lower reaches of many river valleys, the best being those of the Dart, Teign, Meavy and Walkham valleys. These woods extend off the uplands into the steep gorges where the rivers leave the granite plateau and sink through the 'in-country' towards lowland Devon. To the forester they must be anathema, for the shallow soil restricts the timber severely and it is exceptional to find any trees of respectable size and girth. Indeed, almost the only form of commercial exploitation has been the regular coppicing of some of the valleys, the poles being felled at about ten-year intervals, the bark used in tanning and the poles then burned for charcoal in kilns erected on the spot. Both these products having been superseded, the woods are no longer economic, and they are either left untouched, or in a few places have been felled and the land replanted in conifers. But these old oakwoods, whether formerly coppiced or no, are delightful places and full of natural interest. The eye is enchanted with the tracery of trunk and bough and foliage, the brilliant pattern of green or russet and gold of the leaves blending with the infinitely varied soft hues of the lacework of lichens on the branches and boles, and contrasting with the bolder outlines of the rocks which form the ultimate substrate of the wood. To the ear come the sounds of the wind in the tops, of the soft tumble of water in the stream and of the mewing of buzzards which are always about overhead. Such retreats from the frenzied harrying of modern existence are all too infrequent to be spared (Plate 5).

The replacement of oaks by conifers and the planting of these soft-woods on the open moors is a development which has been imposed by considerations of national economy and security, following the devastation of all our woodlands during the First World War. It is inevitable that this has brought about, and continues to effect, marked changes in the character of an area like Dartmoor. So, too, did the advent of Bronze Age man, of the rabbits which the Normans let loose, of the ponies which went feral, of the sheep and cattle which are stocked in ever-increasing numbers. So, too, did the tin-workers, the commoners and farmers of the ancient tenements, the creators of roads, and the builders of bridges. It must be accepted that we humans cannot live our pattern of life without destroying some things and creating others about us. The naturalist at least has lost little and gained much through these conifer plantings on Dartmoor. Their attraction for birds is great in a relatively tree-less land, as is shown by Mr. Spooner's reconnaissances and by the reports of Mr. Hurrell and Mr. Robinson. In particular such fine birds as Montagu's harrier and black game may be encouraged, and it is possible that recent renewal of breeding on the part of the golden plover may also have been favoured by the changed conditions. Other changes in fauna remain to be assessed, but it is probably true to say that the plantings on erstwhile open moorland add to rather than detract from the total interest, and so provide some compensation for the undoubted restrictions they impose on access, and for the changes they have wrought in the landscape. Nevertheless it is legitimate to hope that no further large acreage of moor will be given over to trees, and certainly that no more of the valley oaks will be felled to make way for conifers.

The three upland copses are fascinating places to which all too little space can be devoted. The reader who is interested in them must be referred to discussions in the literature cited at the end of this chapter. It is probable that they represent parts of the indigenous woodland of the Moor, and historical records indicate them to be many hundreds of years old. The individual trees, all pedunculate oaks (*Quercus robur*), stunted and fantastically gnarled as they are, have many of them reached an age of several centuries. By far the most interesting of the three copses is Wistman's Wood, where the density of both the undercover and also the epiphytic growth of mosses, lichens and ferns on the boles and boughs of the trees reaches phenomenal proportions in so windswept a countryside. The ecology of the copse and the contrasts it offers with Black Tor Beare and Piles Copse present enigmas which have yet to be solved, but work in progress may eventually throw light on the problem. These woods are of interest at any time of the year, but particularly so when they are in the variegated splendour of their young spring foliage. Then the leaves of the different trees glow in brilliant shades of green, yellow, bronze and red. Then, too, the wood warbler has come, the grey wagtail is in his breeding plumage, the whole Moor is stirring with life, and the impact of it on the senses is unforgettable.

This account of the natural history of Dartmoor must be completed with a brief reference to its waters. Because the land escaped glaciation it is notably devoid of natural lakes and tarns. The only large bodies of standing water are the artificial reservoirs: Burrator, Holne Moor, Fernworthy, Hennock in the 'in-country' south of Moretonhampstead, the Avon undertaking below Huntingdon Warren, and the Meldon reservoir. The environs of some of these have been planted with trees, and they provide an attractive sanctuary for many waterfowl. Some species of ducks now breed regularly, and many others occur as frequent winter visitors. The innumerable streams of Dartmoor tumble down their upland valleys through series of cascades and pools, and finally leave the Moor through deep gorges cut in the softer rocks of the metamorphic aureole (Plate 3). All too little is known about the fauna of these streams. They carry good fishing; in the Teign, Dart, Taw and Plym there are strong runs of salmon, fostered by conservation, and trout abound in all but the tiniest trickles. In the upper reaches the population of insect nymphs and the like is restricted, by the force of the water, to crevices, the undersides of rocks and stones and to the sparse mosses clinging to the downstream sides of boulders. But in the gorge sections the flow has usually been artificially slowed by the construction of weirs in order to take off leats (open watercourses) for various human purposes. Above the weir is created a stretch of deepish, slow-moving water where sand and gravel are deposited on the bottom. Below the weir there accumulates a delta of rocks, stones and plant remains swept over the barrier during winter spates. Here then a much richer fauna occurs, which may include many species of mayfly, stonefly and caddis, flatworms, leeches, water shrimps and slaters, mites, fresh-water limpets and even such large bivalves as the fresh-water pearl mussel, three parts buried in coarse sand. Dragonfly nymphs creep over the muddy patches or cling among the weeds, while their imagos fly over the water, preying, together with other predacious insects and birds, on the perfect stages of the other insect members of the bottom fauna as they emerge. Whether wading in the deep water, probing the sand and gravel, turning over the shillets in the trickles of the delta, beating and sweeping the vegetation on the banks, or even merely sitting and contemplating and observing, the naturalist will find these weirs abundantly rewarding.

It is quite plain that this has been the merest sketch of Dartmoor's natural history. Much has been omitted, much indeed has still to be discovered and recorded. Those who wish to know more of the plants and animals within the National Park must therefore consult some of the works listed below. But above all they should go in leisure to the Moor itself, and walk and sit quietly there. Only so can a real knowledge of its nature be obtained, and in the doing they will find infinite pleasure.

SELECT BIBLIOGRAPHY

CHRISTY, M. and WORTH, R. H. Ancient Dwarfed Oak Woods of Dartmoor. *Transactions of the Devonshire Association.* 54: 291–342. 1922.

Devon Bird Watching and Preservation Society, Annual Reports. Exeter. 1929–72.

D'URBAN, W. S. M. and MATHEW, M. A. *The Birds of Devon* (2nd Edition). London. 1895.

Earldom of Cornwall: Ministers' Accounts of the Earldom of Cornwall 1296–7, *Camden Society, 3rd Series* Vol. LXVII. Royal Historical Society. 1945.

HARRIS, G. T. Ecological Notes on Wistman's Wood and Black Tor Copse. *Transactions of the Devonshire Association.* 53: 232–45. 1921.

HARRIS, G. T. An Ecological Reconnaissance of Dartmoor. *Transactions of the Devonshire Association.* 70: 37–55. 1938.

HARVEY, L. A. and GORDON, D. ST. L. *Dartmoor.* London. 1953.

MARTIN, W. K. and FRASER, G. T. *Flora of Devon.* Arbroath. 1939.

PAGE, W. *The Victoria History of the Counties of England. Devon.* Vol. 1. London. 1906.

SIMMONDS, I. G. (ed.). *Dartmoor Essays.* Devonshire Association. 1964. Contains essays on botany, soils, and ecology of the Moor.

STIDSTON, S. T. *A List of the Lepidoptera of Devon.* Pt. I and Introduction. Torquay, Torquay Times & Devonshire Press. 1952.

TANSLEY, A. G. *The British Islands and their Vegetation.* Cambridge. 1939.

PLATE 5. The interior of Wistman's Wood

PLATE 6. The East Dart on the central plateau

PLATE 7. Bog cotton on the central peat bog

PLATE 8. A Dartmoor buzzard at the nest

PLATE 9. Spinster's Rock near Drewsteignton

PLATE 10. Kistvaen at Roundy Park near Postbridge

PLATE 11. Grey Wethers stone circles

PLATE 12. Hut circle at Grimspound

3

Prehistoric Monuments on Dartmoor

BY AILEEN FOX

Senior Lecturer in British Archaeology, University of Exeter

ON the granite upland of Dartmoor there is a unique assembly of pre-historic antiquities: no one of them can compare in size or grandeur with monuments like Stonehenge, Maeshowe, or Maiden Castle, but because they are so numerous, and because their setting is relatively unchanged since prehistoric times, they provide a clear, full and intelligible picture of early man in relation to his environment. A walk up the upper reaches of the Plym or Avon, an exploration of the flanks of the East Dart or North Teign rivers, for instance, will reveal to the discerning visitor an impressive succession of settlements, as well as groups of monuments that indicate the traditional religious centres of early man.

This massing of monuments can be accounted for in two ways: in the first place the moorland mass provides a broad tract of well-watered country, standing for the most part above the tree line, and so well suited to sustain a primitive pastoral economy. Hills so dominating, so widespreading and so inviting would act like a magnet for invaders enter-ing the South Devon estuaries and induce them to push through the forests, which covered much of the lower land in early times. Secondly, the use of granite as a building material accounts for the survival of many prehistoric structures, which elsewhere, built in timber, have left no surface trace. Since relatively little settlement or industrial development has taken place on Dartmoor in historic times, an unusually high proportion of these stone-built monuments survive to the present day.

This section of the Guide is intended to provide a conspectus of the monuments that will be encountered in the National Park, arranged as far as possible in chronological order; but since little modern scientific excavation has taken place, many uncertainties still remain. Some indica-tion will also be given of sites that are especially worth visiting, although many of these are accessible only to good walkers and map readers. (See pp. 23–25.)

The earliest structures on Dartmoor, as opposed to chance finds of flint and other stone implements, are megalithic tombs (known also as dolmens or cromlechs) which date from the Neolithic or New Stone Age, between 3000 and 2000 B.C. These, when originally completed, consisted of a burial chamber built above ground of large upright slabs (orthostats) and roofed with another (the capstone), the whole concealed beneath a long cairn or mound. They were communal tombs, in which the bones of successive generations were interred and at which religious rites and ceremonies were carried out. Their builders were a people who reached Britain by sea in successive groups from the Atlantic coasts of France and Spain, and who colonized our western seaboards. Only three or four tombs occur on Dartmoor, distributed on the margin. The best example is near South Brent, where a cairn, 130 feet long, with the tumbled uprights of the chamber protruding through the turf, can be seen on the skyline, set axially on the saddle between Corringdon Ball and Brent Fore Hill. At Spinster's Rock, in farmland near Drewsteignton, only the great capstone perched on three uprights remains (Plate 9), but as the monument was re-erected after collapse in 1862, the original form is uncertain.

With the coming of the Beaker folk about 1700 B.C., individual burial replaced the communal vault, and this change is probably first reflected on Dartmoor in the building of large stone cists, rectangular structures sunk below ground level, covered by a low round cairn and big enough to hold a body in a flexed position: examples can be seen at Merrivale or at Roundy Park above Postbridge (Plate 10). When cremation of the dead became the general burial rite, the cist was reduced to a box-like structure, little more than 3 feet by 2 feet internally, but large enough to hold the cremated bones, personal possessions such as a bronze knife-dagger, and an offering of food or drink in a pottery vessel. The graves on Dartmoor are usually marked by a low cairn not more than 20 feet in diameter, sometimes edged with large stones and inconspicuously sited on the hill-slopes. The Beaker folk were newcomers to Britain, landing in bands on our southern and eastern coasts from different parts of northern France, Holland and Germany, from 1900 B.C. onwards and spreading rapidly across the country. They are named from their distinctive fine ornamented red pottery, the Beaker, examples of which have been found in graves near Chagford, at Fernworthy and Watern Down: these are now in the Plymouth Museum.

To this initial phase of the Bronze Age it is usual to ascribe the erection of the free-standing Stone Circles on Dartmoor: the uprights are usually between 3 feet and 5 feet high, set well apart, and enclose a level area from 60 feet to 110 feet in diameter. Excavation has shown that within the ring fires have been lit leaving a scatter of ashes and charcoal, but that no burial has taken place. It seems reasonable to suppose that these were sacred sites, where ritual was carried out, akin to the great sarsen circles at Avebury or Stonehenge. The largest and most impressive of the twelve Dartmoor examples are the Grey Wethers (Plate 11), two circles set side by side on the flat summit (1,500 feet) of the ridge dividing the South Teign and East Dart valleys. A more accessible example is Scorhill above the North Teign river at its junction with the Walla Brook; here the largest stone is 8 feet high and some of the stones are unusually close-set. These free-standing circles should not be confused with the ring of uprights or peristalith that margin or form part of certain small cairns on Dartmoor, or that act as retaining circles or kerbs; a typical example can be seen by the roadside on Soussons Common.

Other Dartmoor monuments that imply a religious use are the Stone Rows, also known as Avenues or Alignments, which are a speciality of this region and suggest a culture developed in isolation over a long period of time. The rows are nearly all associated with burials in small cairns (Plate 14). A typical example can be seen on Watern Hill, on Chagford Common, one mile north-east of Warren House Inn. Here fifty pairs of small stones, about 3 feet high, aligned in two rows 6 feet apart, breast the slope towards a low cairn, 20 feet in diameter. The stones nearest the cairn are larger than the others in the rows: at the lower end there is a large slab set transversely, the so-called Blocking-stone terminal. The rows here, as elsewhere, give the impression of a ceremonial way to a tomb, of a width suitable only for one or two votaries to approach at a time. In other instances, the rows lead up from the side of a stream, as from the Meavy at Hartor; at Challacombe, behind Headland Warren Farm, three rows lead up to a menhir, an isolated pillar-stone, which may mark a burial place. Other rows in the Erme valley, which are single and lead to cairns on the upper slopes of Butterdon, Greenhill and Stallmoor, are very extensive, each over a mile long: their purpose has not been determined. The most dramatic row is on Stalldon, between the Erme and Yealm, which is built of exceptionally large stones and is visible on the 1,300-foot hill-top from many directions.

There are sixty of these remarkable monuments widely distributed on the Moor but many of them occur in groups. At Merrivale, just south of the Princetown road, there are two double rows aligned across a flat-topped bluff; nearby is a free-standing circle of tiny stones, a menhir or standing stone, a large cist and several cairns: the whole assembly gives the impression of a sacred spot hallowed by prolonged use. The same impressive massing of sepulchral monuments can be seen at Drizzle-combe in the upper Plym valley, where standing stones, menhirs, form striking terminals to the three rows, or the five rows on Shovel Down, near Kestor.

The large grey round cairns that are conspicuous on many of the Dartmoor skylines also mark the burial places of Bronze Age man. Some-times they congregate to form a cemetery as that on the top of Butterdon Hill (1,200 feet) near Ivybridge, where the largest measures 100 feet in diameter and still stands 12 feet high. More often they are spaced out along a natural traffic way, on a ridge such as Hamel Down (1,700 feet), in contrast to the small cairns and rows that are normally to be found on the hill-slopes. Unfortunately the majority have been disturbed by tomb-robbers in the past and reduced to a tumbled heap around a hole, at the bottom of which the slabs of a cist may be visible. A typical Middle Bronze Age urn containing cremated bones was excavated from such a cairn on Hurston Ridge, Chagford, and is now in the Plymouth Museum; in date it is about 1300–1000 B.C.

It is time now to turn from the sepulchral monuments to the pre-historic settlements on Dartmoor. Three kinds can be distinguished, the Pounds, the Villages and the Farmsteads; in each the inhabitants lived in round huts, built of drystone granite walling.

The Pounds are walled enclosures. The majority will be found in the southern and western parts of the Moor, occupying the slopes between 1,000 and 1,300 feet of the valleys of the Avon, Erme, Yealm, Plym and Meavy. They vary in size and strength as well as in the numbers and sizes of huts they contain. The best known is Grimspound (Plate 12) which lies in a fold of the hills at 1,500 feet between Hamel Down and Hookney Tor, near Manaton. Here twenty-four small huts are enclosed by a massive wall 9 feet thick and 6 feet high, constructed with a core of small stone between faces of large boulders. Grim's Lake, a stream, flows through the north side of the enclosure: the entrance to the pound is on the opposite and upper side, by an impressive paved passage-way through the thickness of the walls. The situation of the pound, which is not defensible, and its relation to the stream, indicate that the settlement was built by pastoralists, anxious to water their stock and to protect them against wild beasts. Typical of the many smaller sites are the five pounds at Trowlesworthy Warren, each containing a group of five to ten huts. A pastoral economy is manifest at Riders' Rings, a large double enclosure in the Avon valley, where in addition to the huts there are numerous courtyards attached to the pound wall which look like places for stalling cattle.

The Villages consist of complexes of small huts, usually 10 to 20 feet in diameter, linked by low wandering stone walls which form irregular enclosures. No rational plan is apparent: some of the enclosures were probably cultivation plots, others paddocks or pens for stock. As many as sixty-eight huts make up the settlement on Standon Down near Willsworthy in the Tavy valley and forty-five on Langstone Moor in the upper Walkham valley (both in the Military Danger Zone); other settle-ments of this type are to be found on the south and west sides of the Moor.

The Farmsteads are distributed mainly on the south-eastern side of the Moor, from Throwleigh Common to Holne Moor. They are

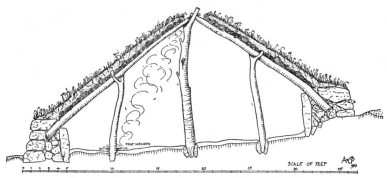

FIG. I. Reconstructed section of hut at Kes Tor

indicated by the remains of small rectilinear fields usually associated with one to four isolated huts; the fields are separated from each other by a row of upright slabs and by slight plough terraces (lynchets). The huts are larger (20 to 30 feet diameter) and more massively built than those in the Pounds or Villages. Typical examples can be seen near the main road on Bush Down or Shapley Common near Postbridge and on Yar Tor Down near Dartmeet. Excavation has shown that the roofs of turf or thatch were supported on a ring of timber uprights and a centre post (Fig. I): the hearth was towards the back of the hut and part of the floor and the narrow entrance was paved and sometimes screened by a low external wall from the south-west wind. The discovery of saddle querns confirms that their inhabitants were arable farmers. At Kestor near Chagford, Foales Arrishes near Widecombe and elsewhere, several holdings related to small hut groups have coalesced to form a regular and extensive field system, which shows up well on air-photographs.

It is uncertain at what period in the Bronze Age this varied and intensive settlement of Dartmoor began, though there can be little doubt that it was well established during the Middle Bronze Age, *circa* 1200 B.C. This is because the acid soil of the Moor destroys all dateable metal objects that would provide a time-scale. The crude handmade pottery with incised decoration found in the huts is similar to that from Middle Bronze Age settlements recently excavated in Cornwall at Gwithian and St. Eval. The Farmsteads, however, were still in existence in the early Iron Age (450–250 B.C.), for at Kestor an iron-smelting furnace was discovered. There is no conclusive evidence that the hut dwellers exploited the other rich mineral deposits, tin and copper, of the Moor. The settlements, like the burials, give the impression of a long period of occupation, and of a self-sufficient economy capable of being sustained in isolation for a very long time.

Finally, on the foothills and on the edges of the Moor, there are the defended settlements, the hill-forts (marked as *camps* or *castles* on maps), characteristic of the later Iron Age. These are the fortifications of various groups of Celtic peoples drawn from the Marne, Seine and Breton districts of France, who invaded Britain from the third century B.C. onwards. Those in Devon and Cornwall belonged to a confederacy later known to the Romans as the Dumnonii. Seizing on a natural strong point, a hill-top such as Cranbrook (1,105 feet) near Moretonhampstead, they ringed it with ditches and stout ramparts, from which the inhabitants defended themselves by sling stones and other missiles. Wherever possible, advantage was taken of natural defences such as the steep sides of a spur or a ravine. At Prestonbury, near Drewsteignton, the precipitous slopes to the Teign at Fingle Bridge were incorporated in the circuit of the ramparts; at Dewerstone, it was only necessary to construct two stone walls across the neck of the promontory above the junction of the Plym and Meavy rivers, which run in deep wooded valleys below the fort.

Some hill-forts were built as the dwelling-place for a chieftain and his people; others as a refuge in time of inter-tribal wars. Until the coming of the Romans, siege tactics such as Caesar described were not employed, consequently it was not essential to have a water supply within the defences. The main object of attack was the entrance, where the arrangement of the ramparts shows ingenious devices to place the assailants at a disadvantage: at Prestonbury and at East Hill, a small promontory fort near Okehampton, the rampart ends are incurved towards the gate, forming a bottle-neck under fire from both sides. The large-scale effort involved in constructing these citadels shows the growing resources and political power of the Celtic warrior-rulers.

It remains uncertain when the prehistoric settlements on Dartmoor and its periphery came to an end. There is no evidence as yet for contact between the builders of the huts and the hill-forts, which have now been described. It is known that soon after the Roman military conquest of A.D. 43–50 the territory of the Dumnonii became one of the cantons of the new province, administered by a Romano-British civil government from the capital city at Exeter (*Isca Dumnoniorum*). We have yet to learn whether the country folk continued to live in their old haunts in the upland as they did under the Roman military régime in Wales and northern England, or moved to new settlements on the Moor; or whether, at any time, the Dartmoor hills were deserted.

BIBLIOGRAPHY

BRAILSFORD, J. W. Bronze Age stone monuments on Dartmoor. *Antiquity*. 1938.

FOX, AILEEN. Celtic fields and farms on Dartmoor. *Proceedings of the Prehistoric Society*. 1955.

FOX, AILEEN. *South-West England* (Ancient People and Places). 1964. A general account of the archaeology of the region.

RADFORD, C. A. R. Early settlement on Dartmoor and the Cornish moors. *Proceedings of the Prehistoric Society*. 1952.

WORTH, R. H. *Dartmoor*. Plymouth, 1953. A useful compendium of articles previously published in *Transactions of Devonshire Association* and elsewhere.

CLASSIFIED LIST OF PREHISTORIC MONUMENTS
ESPECIALLY WORTH VISITING

The monuments are a personal selection and have been chosen to cover a wide range of varieties and locations: some are concealed by bracken in summer. For description and chronology see Chapter 3.

A National Grid reference to the 1-inch Ordnance Survey Map is given for each site, following the sheet number in parentheses, i.e. 175, Okehampton; 187, Plymouth. The directions are indications of the easiest route for visitors unfamiliar with the Moor. It is dangerous to enter a Military Firing Zone when the red flag is flying. Walkers are advised to take a map and compass.

(1) *Megaliths, Stone Circles and Standing Stones*

Beardown Man, Devil's Tor. Standing stone. (187) 596/797. In military danger area. Across Moor from Beardown near Two Bridges, 3½ miles.

Corringdon Ball, South Brent. Megalithic tomb with long cairn. (188) 670/613, marked as Kistvaen. Footpath to Ball Gate from Aish, 1½ miles.

Grey Wethers. Two stone circles, re-erected. (175) 639/832. Over the Moor from Postbridge, via Hartland Tor and White Ridge, 3 miles.

Langstone Moor, Peter Tavy. Stone circle. (187) 558/782. In military danger area. Accessible by track from Peter Tavy to White Tor, and thence 1 mile across Moor.

Ringmoor Down, Sheepstor. Stone circle, re-erected. (187) 564/655. By-road to Brisworthy, footpath ¼ mile.

Scorhill, Gidleigh. Stone circle. (175) 655/873. Footpath from Berrydown, or from Batworthy crossing River Teign by footbridge, 1 mile.

Spinster's Rock, Drewsteignton. Megalithic tomb chamber, restored. (175) 700/908. In field, Shilstone farm, private property: visible from road.

(2) *Stone Rows, Cairns and Cists. Bronze Age*

Butterdon Hill, Harford. Group of six large cairns. (187) 660/587. Footpath from Bittaford Bridge or across the Moor from Wrangaton golf course, $1\frac{1}{2}$ miles.

Challacombe. Stone rows and standing stone. (175) 690/809. Footpath from Headland Warren Farm or Warren House Inn (B 3212), south of old mine workings, 1 mile.

Drizzlecombe, Ditsworthy Warren. Group of three stone rows, cairns and standing stones. (187) 591/670. From Sheepstor to Burracombe, thence by track across Moor to Ditsworthy Warren and up the Plym valley, 1 mile.

Merrivale. Group of three stone rows, cairns, large cist, stone circle and standing stone. (187) 554/748. On south side of Princetown–Tavistock main road, A 384.

Roundy Park, Postbridge. Cairn and large cist. (175) 639/797. On west side of River Dart, 1 mile above Postbridge.

Shovel Down, Chagford. Group of five stone rows, cairns and a standing stone; one cairn has four internal rings of stone uprights. (175) 650/860. By-road to Batworthy, via Thorn, $\frac{1}{2}$ mile across Moor.

Stalldon, Cornwood. Stone row and cairn. (187) 633/624. By-road from Cornwood to Stall Moor reservoir, near Yadsworthy, 1 mile across Moor to summit.

Stall Moor, Cornwood. Stone row and circle; row extends for 1 mile to Erme valley, where it crosses the river and the Red Lake stream and then ascends Greenhill to summit cairn, total distance $2\frac{1}{2}$ miles. (187) 635/644. Across Moor from Stall Moor reservoir, 3 miles.

Soussons Common, Postbridge. Cairn, denuded, with cist and marginal circle. (175) 676/778. On roadside, Postbridge–Widecombe road.

Watern Down, Chagford Common. Stone rows and cairn. (175) 675/825. Footpath from Warren House Inn, (B 3212) 1 mile.

Yellowmead, Sheepstor. Cairn, denuded, with four internal rings of stone uprights. (187) 574/667, marked as stone circle. By-road from Sheepstor, $\frac{1}{4}$ mile across Moor.

(3) *Settlements. Bronze–Iron Age*

Broadun Ring, Postbridge. Nine small huts in massively walled enclosure (Pound). (175) 637/802, marked as camp. On west flank of East Dart valley, $1\frac{1}{2}$ miles from Postbridge.

PLATE 13. Old tin-workings at Vitifer near Warren House Inn

PLATE 14. Stone row at Down Tor

Foales Arrishes, Widecombe. Eight large huts with extensive field system, partly remade in medieval and later times. (175) 737/758. Across Moor from Hemsworthy gate, ¼ mile.

Grimspound, Manaton. Twenty-four small huts in walled enclosure. (175) 700/809. Footpath from Shapley Common–Widecombe road, opposite Headland Warren Farm.

Kestor, Chagford. Twelve large huts and extensive field system: one hut in small enclosure, Roundy Pound. (175) 665/867. On by-road to Batworthy via Thorn, and north-east of Kestor.

Langstone Moor, Walkham valley. Open village settlement, forty-five huts. (175) 556/779. Military danger zone. Accessible via White Tor, and thence 1 mile across Moor.

Little Mistor, Walkham valley. Open village settlement, thirty-three huts in two groups. (175) 555/765. Across Moor on east flank of Walkham valley from Merrivale, 1 mile.

Riders' Rings, South Brent. A double-walled enclosure, containing numerous huts and animal pens. (187) 680/645. By-road to Shipley Bridge; across Moor via Black Tor, above River Avon, 1½ miles.

Shapley Common. Seven large huts with fields, two farm groups. (175) 695/824. On either side of road to Widecombe.

Standon Down, Tavy valley. Open village settlement, sixty-eight huts. (175) 554/824. Military danger zone. Accessible by rough road to Baggator, thence across Moor, 2 miles.

Trowlesworthy. Group of eight walled enclosures, each containing five to ten huts. (187) 573/645. Footpath to Trowlesworthy Warren Farm, and thence across Moor, 1¼ miles.

(4) *Hill-forts. Iron Age*

Cranbrook Castle, Moretonhampstead. Hill-fort, stone-faced inner rampart, berm, and ditch, with small second bank and ditch on south: entrance on east. North side not completed. (175) 739/890. By-road from Moretonhampstead, or track from Fingle Bridge, Teign valley.

Hembury Castle, Buckfastleigh. Hill-fort, with single rampart and deep ditch: the mound inside probably an earlier (Bronze Age) cairn or barrow. (187) 726/684. On Buckfast–Holne road, National Trust.

Prestonbury, Drewsteignton. Hill-fort with three lines of wide-spaced ramparts, ending on steep scarp to River Teign, forming triple enclosures: a fine inturned entrance on east side. (175) 746/900. By-road to Preston farm, footpath ¼ mile.

C

4

Dartmoor from Roman Times to the Present Day

BY W. G. HOSKINS

Formerly Reader in Economic History in the University of Oxford

THE history of man on Dartmoor begins, as Lady Fox has shown in the preceding chapter, at some unknown point in the Bronze Age, and this first phase—the prehistoric—comes to an end about the time of the Roman conquest of south-western England, round about A.D. 50. Whether men continued to live on the inclement moorland during and after the Roman period is still not known. The absence of any archaeological data in this period is not conclusive proof of the absence of man, for a primitive and thinly-settled native economy may well have perished without leaving any material traces, especially in the acid soils of the Moor.

Some slight evidence afforded by stream-names on the Moor suggests that a few descendants of Iron Age farmers may have continued to live in the more sheltered valleys. No fewer than four streams (tributaries of the Dart, Teign, Tavy and Avon) are called Walla Brook, and at least two of these (and probably the others also) derive from the Old English words *Weala brōc*, meaning 'the stream of the Welsh, i.e. the Britons'. This suggests that when the first Saxons penetrated as far as the Dartmoor foothills, probably in the seventh and eighth centuries, they were aware of British peasant farmers living in hamlets along the higher reaches of these moorland streams.

It is possible that the remote farmsteads of Babeny and Pizwell, high up the Walla Brook that joins the East Dart, represent two such Celtic hamlets. They are not recorded by name until 1260, at which date they were hamlets, probably of three farmsteads each. Since that date they have shrunk to one farmstead each. We cannot definitely assert that they were of Celtic or British origin, but the stream-name, coupled with the remarkable pattern of small square fields at Babeny (especially on the east side of the Walla Brook), strongly suggests this possibility. The fields around farmsteads of medieval origin (twelfth to thirteenth centuries) are small but exceedingly irregular in shape, the characteristic pattern of reclamation from the open moor at this period.

Babeny may be reached from Dartmeet (on the Two Bridges–Ashburton road) by following the lane to Brimps and thence the path beside the East Dart and up the Walla Brook. To reach Pizwell one may either continue the walk up the Walla Brook, or walk from Postbridge on the Two Bridges–Exeter road.

Further evidence of the antiquity and early importance of Babeny is shown in the fact that it possessed a water-mill in 1302, then described as 'newly built', and that all dwellers in the Forest of Dartmoor were obliged to grind their corn at this mill. Lest we are surprised at corn being grown on medieval Dartmoor, it may be said that in 1627 (when there was a lawsuit) the mill was described as standing 'in the farthest parts of the Parish of Lydford, near the wild wastes, [in] good land, inhabited with rich inhabitants, and tilled with oats and rye, and with manurance tilled with barley'.

Dartmoor is not mentioned by name in Domesday Book (1086). We first hear of the name *Dertemora* in a record of 1181, but that is not to say that it was valueless and unknown in earlier generations. It is certain that the Saxons, like prehistoric men before them, made use of the vast areas of common pasture which the Moor afforded to those settled in villages and hamlets around its borders. In later times the right to pasture animals on the Moor was restricted to the adjacent parishes and hamlets, for which right they paid a special rent known as *venville*. (For fuller details of this payment the reader is referred to R. Hansford Worth's *Dartmoor*, pages 342–7.) The word is derived from *fines villarum*, i.e. 'fines of the vills' with pasture rights.

Down to the year 1204 the whole of Devon was regarded as subject to the royal forest laws and preserved for the king's hunting, and hence was technically a 'Forest'. In that year the men of Devon purchased their freedom, at the heavy price of 5,000 marks (equivalent to perhaps £400,000 today), from the burdens and vexations of the forest laws, and the whole county was disafforested except for Dartmoor and Exmoor. Dartmoor therefore remained a forest in law, and is often called such today; but this does not mean that it was ever forested in the modern sense of the word, as Professor Harvey has shown in his chapter on the Natural History of the Moor. It meant only that it was still kept as a royal hunting preserve.

A generation later, in the year 1239, Henry III granted the manor of Lydford and its castle, and the Forest of Dartmoor, to Richard, Earl of Poitou and Cornwall, and from this time onwards the larger part of Dartmoor was among the possessions of the Duchy of Cornwall, as it still is today.

Apart from the summer pastures and possibly a few isolated farming hamlets in the valleys, most of Dartmoor remained unknown to man until about the middle of the twelfth century. Then an important discovery was made. On the south-western foothills of the Moor, probably in the neighbourhood of Sheepstor, hitherto untouched deposits of tin ore were found. In a few years this area became the richest source of tin in Europe. Prospectors and settlers flocked in. For two or three generations there was what we may call a 'Tin Rush', with important consequences for the whole development of Dartmoor and the surrounding country.

First of all, the new prospectors opened up the Moor—or certain valleys at least—and made it known. Many new farms were created in these years (between about 1150 and 1250) on the edge of the Moor, of which Brisworthy in the upper Plym valley is a good example, surrounded by its tiny irregular fields, fields dotted with granite boulders and bounded by granite also, and approached by deep lanes. Slowly the settlers penetrated into many of the southern and western valleys, creating little pastoral farmsteads (with some corn-growing) and founding what became known as the 'ancient tenements', which were eventually thirty-five or more in number. We hear of many farmsteads well into the Moor by the closing years of the thirteenth century and the early years of the fourteenth. This colonization movement ended with the onset of the Black Death (1349) which, oddly enough, was devastating even among the remote farmsteads of Dartmoor. Several of them were left untenanted for a considerable time. The overgrown 'cultivation terraces' above Challacombe (Plate 24) possibly represent medieval fields that were abandoned about this time and never reoccupied.

The tinners left more direct traces of their activities upon the Moor, wherever they 'streamed' their tin. Early tinners used what we should call open-cast workings. Not until about 1500 do we hear of tin-mines with shafts, and most of the tin-mines of which we see abundant remains upon the Moor date from long after that. The deep crevasses formed by the early tinners in their excavations for the precious ore may be seen in many places, best of all perhaps on the hillside above the West Webburn valley (Plate 13).

The great prosperity of the Dartmoor tin trade also led to the growth of several little towns around the edge of the Moor. We hear of new boroughs at Tavistock, Plympton and Ashburton in the second half of the twelfth century, created largely to handle and take advantage of the tin trade. Later these towns became organized as the Stannary Towns (from the Latin word *stannum*, tin), to which all the moorland tin had to be brought for assaying and weighing, stamping, and payment of duty to the Crown. On the eastern side of the Moor, as tin-working developed in that quarter, the village of Chagford was elevated to the status of Stannary Town, so making four in all.

The stannaries were a source of great profit to the Crown and were a protected industry. They were governed by their own strict code of laws, and offenders against these laws were committed to a special prison at Lydford. This prison still stands, though it is known today as Lydford Castle, a massive and impressive monument built in 1195.

Other relics of this ancient industry which may be seen upon the Moor are the remains of the blowing-houses where the tin ore was smelted upon the spot before being carried down to the stannary town (Plate 15). These smelting-houses were built crudely of surface granite and used charcoal as a fuel, and many of them can be found by the visitor who searches carefully. Several are marked upon the 2½-inch Ordnance maps. For fuller details of these interesting structures, reference should be made to R. H. Worth's *Dartmoor*, which contains a chapter upon the subject.

The simultaneous development of farming and of the tin trade upon the Moor produced other changes in the Dartmoor landscape, notably the creation of primitive roads or trackways, and of equally primitive bridges, on the Moor and its foothills. Here there is much for the visitor to see, not comparable in quantity with the galaxy of prehistoric monuments but all intensely interesting and much of it unique in England.

The main road which now crosses the entire width of the Moor from north-east to south-west (B 3212) probably originated in the thirteenth century with the greater movement of tinners and farmers. It was no more than a lonely, unmade trackway upon which it was all too easy to lose one's way, and it seems very likely that the crude granite crosses that one sees at certain points on the Moor and its approach roads were set up at this time to act as silent guide-posts.

Some of these crosses were also set up as boundary points. Bennett's Cross, beside the main road from Moretonhampstead to Princetown, about half a mile from the Warren House Inn, is a good example of such a cross (Plate 18); and another fine example is Marchant's Cross, just south-east of Meavy village. Much more isolated are two crosses standing beside a trackway running roughly southwards from Princetown towards Plym Head. One of these is now called Nun's Cross: probably a fanciful modern name derived from the ineradicable popular belief that medieval monks, nuns, and abbots spent a good deal of time wandering about on Dartmoor. Nun's Cross was for centuries called Siward's Cross. It was a boundary mark as early as 1240, and it almost certainly dates from the year 1204 when the metes and bounds of the Forest of Dartmoor must have been carefully demarcated, following the disafforestation of the remainder of Devon. Marchant's Cross may have been set up at the same time.

The clapper bridges, constructed of massive flat slabs of granite, almost certainly date from the thirteenth century also. Although they bear at first sight a prehistoric appearance, this primitive style of construction persisted for many centuries owing to the intractable nature of the building material. The most notable, and the most accessible, of these bridges is that over the East Dart at Postbridge; and there are less striking examples at Dartmeet, at Bellever, and over the Cherry Brook between Postbridge and Two Bridges. Several others may be located with the aid of the 1-inch or 2½-inch maps (Plate 22).

The medieval colonists of Dartmoor and its fringes found the surface of the land littered with granite blocks of all shapes and sizes. Such surface granite was known as 'moorstone'.* Before they could cultivate any fields, or even pasture stock in them, tons of stone had to be shifted. This stone was used to construct the loose walling that marked off one field from another, and also for the building of the first peasant farmsteads. Since the material was so massive and indestructible, several of these early farmsteads survive, in part at least (Fig. 2). There is no other

---

* Granite was not quarried on Dartmoor until the early nineteenth century. Until that date the surface granite was ample for all needs.

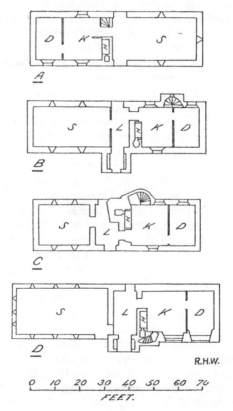

FIG. 2. Some plans of early Dartmoor farmhouses

region in England where we can still study the plan and construction of early medieval peasant farmsteads as one can on Dartmoor and its fringes. The best surviving examples are those at Yardworthy (Plate 19) and Yeo (both in Chagford parish), at Challacombe (in the valley below Grimspound), and at Cudlipp Town and Cholwich Town just off the Moor, near Tavistock and Cornwood respectively. Other good examples may be seen behind the present farmhouse at Clannaborough (in Throw-

EARLY TYPES OF DARTMOOR HOUSE

The following brief notes relating to the house-plans on the opposite page are designed to help visitors to Dartmoor to understand the elements of the development of these interesting houses from medieval times onwards. They are far from exhaustive and are intended only as a rough guide to the subject, which deserves a book to itself.

A. Here dwelling-house and shippen together form a simple rectangle, though the house-part is self-contained within four walls. Men and animals used a common entrance into the shippen, the entrance into the house being through the side-wall which also contained the single massive hearth. (K = kitchen or living-room, H = hearth, D = dairy, S = shippen). Good examples of this type may be seen at Collihole in Chagford parish, and at Higher Godsworthy in Peter Tavy, though there may be minor variations in the positions of the stairway.

B. In this type a wooden partition is added on the shippen side, so that a large lobby (L) is formed between shippen and house. This lobby is still used by men and animals alike. A massive newel stair in the back wall leads to upper rooms, which were generally formed between 1570 and 1640 by ceiling over the lower rooms.

C. Here a masonry wall is substituted for the wooden partition dividing shippen and lobby. The lobby was usually made wider with this development (as at Old Bellever). The shippen is often found to have been converted into a parlour at a later date, with a bedroom over. This was a fundamental change in the cultural history of the Dartmoor house, for it displaced the animals from their age-old status in the house itself to a shippen in the yard. It may have occurred generally on Dartmoor during the course of the eighteenth century, probably as early as Queen Anne's time in good yeoman houses like Lower Tor in Widecombe parish (Plate 16) and much more recently in the more remote and backward houses. No farmhouse survives on Dartmoor in which men and animals are still housed under the same roof, though the original plan of such houses can frequently be seen. Good examples of types B and C are represented by Warne's Kitchen at the back of Easton Town in Sampford Spiney parish, and by Higher Shapley in Chagford parish before the porch was added in 1776.

D. Here the animals are excluded from the common entrance and lobby. A separate doorway is provided to the shippen beside the original common doorway, and the latter is adorned with a more or less elaborate porch in granite, and reserved for the family. Shilstone in Throwleigh parish (dated 1656) is a good example of this type, and so too is Lower Tor in Widecombe, where the porch is dated 1707. At Hole in Chagford the porch was added in 1668 to an older house. At Lower Tor the medieval shippen end of the house is still plain to see, though no longer used as such. It is entered by an arched doorway of late fifteenth-century date, and the shell of the house as a whole is of this period.

leigh parish) and at Neadon (see page 62 under Manaton). In all these instances a more modern house has been built near by, and the ancestral house has been abandoned as a dwelling and put to some other use.

Apart from these survivals of medieval farmhouses, the student of peasant houses will find a great deal of later building to interest him. Many of the original Dartmoor farmhouses were rebuilt between the early seventeenth century and the early eighteenth, and represent what

FIG. 3. Sherberton farm as it was

is often thought of as the 'typical' moorland farmhouse. Good examples abound in the large parishes of Chagford and Widecombe especially (Plates 16, 17, and Fig. 3), but no moorland parish is without some attractive building of this happy period. Those who wish for further guidance will find Worth's essay on The Dartmoor House (published in his *Dartmoor*) most helpful and enlightening, and reference should also be made to the gazetteer at the end of this Guide.

In recent years we have begun to find the remains of abandoned medieval villages—perhaps hamlets would be a better word—on the Moor. The best of these lies between Hound Tor and Great Tor, just above a line of springs, about 200 yards north-west of Great Tor (see 2½-inch sheet, sx/77). There seem to be about twelve buildings with

PLATE 15. Remains of (*a*) old blowing-houses near Henglake in the Avon valley; (*b*) lower blowing-house above Merrivale Bridge on the Walkham, showing moulds used by tinners

PLATE 16. Lower Tor farmhouse near Poundsgate

PLATE 17. Detail of porch at Lower Tor

their crofts and associated fields. Since the walls stand only a foot or two above the surface, the site should be visited on a good day in winter or early spring. The houses are clearly early medieval in plan. They appear to be of the 'long house' type, with the family at one end and the cattle at the other. It seems that the village was abandoned at the time of the Black Death.

Before leaving the earlier history of the Moor one should draw attention to the granite churches of the region, some of them noble buildings and none without a considerable interest. The splendid tower of Widecombe church (Plate 20), often called the cathedral of the Moor, is traditionally associated with the prosperous tinners of the parish in the early 1500s, who paid for its building; and this tradition is very likely true. The early fifteenth-century tower of Moretonhampstead is another noble piece of work, and Chagford church is altogether good. Among the smaller churches, those of Throwleigh, Holne, Buckland in the Moor and Lustleigh are particularly worth notice. Several churches contain fine medieval screens.

After the early boom in the tin trade in the twelfth and thirteenth centuries, Dartmoor production fell away to only a fraction of that of Cornwall. During the late fifteenth century and the early sixteenth, however, a second boom occurred, lasting some thirty or forty years, probably the result of the development of shaft-mining which enabled hitherto untouched lodes to be reached. Probably many of the surviving ' blowing-houses' on the Moor date from this time, though some may be older. Thereafter, tin production on Dartmoor fell steadily. In the 1670s the total output of the Moor was barely ten tons a year, as against some 1,500 tons from Cornwall. A certain amount of mining was carried on into the nineteenth century, the last mine to be worked on a commercial scale being the Hen Roost on Holne Moor, which closed down in 1916. More recently a small company called the Birch Tor Tin Mine worked over the tailings of two older mines (Vitifer and Golden Dagger) and sent a few tons of ore every week to South Wales until 1939.

The modern history of Dartmoor begins in 1780 when Mr. Thomas Tyrwhitt (later Sir Thomas) began reclaiming land on the western side of the Moor in his capacity as Lord Warden of the Stannaries. In 1785 a farm was created at Tor Royal, about half a mile south-east of Princetown. A house was built here in 1785–98, added to in 1815–20, and restored by A. E. Richardson in 1912.

Sir Thomas's most notable contribution to the history of Dartmoor, however, was the foundation of the town of Princetown and its prison. Before 1806 nothing stood here, in this bleak and awful spot between two tors. In that year he proposed to the Government that a barracks (or prison) should be built here to house the growing number of prisoners of war, many of whom were then confined in hulks in Plymouth Sound. He felt that the prisoners could be usefully employed in quarrying granite, in building roads, and in opening up parts of the moor for cultivation. A site was given by the then Prince of Wales (hence the name Princetown), who held the lands of the Duchy of Cornwall, and a prison erected in 1806 to the design of Daniel Alexander. Of the five original prison buildings, arranged like the spokes of a wheel, only one survives —the so-called French Prison.

With the end of the Napoleonic Wars, the prison was closed and the little town of Princetown which had grown up around the new quarries languished and probably would have perished had not Sir Thomas also conceived the idea of a railway from Princetown down to Plymouth. This railway was designed to carry down granite from the Moor for export to London and other places, and to return with lime for the sour soils of the upland farms and coal to enable the inhabitants to sustain life during a Dartmoor winter. The Plymouth and Dartmoor Railway was opened in 1823. It carried on for over fifty years with steadily diminishing revenues. In 1880 the Dartmoor portion of the line was reconstructed to take locomotives, and the line was opened from Princetown to Yelverton, where it joined the Plymouth–Tavistock Railway, in 1883. This exceedingly picturesque railway, winding in gigantic curves around the tors up to a height of 1,400 feet above sea level, delighted generations of holiday-makers and also served to carry necessary traffic during other times of the year when the roads are snowbound. The line did not, however, pay its way and was closed down. The last train ran up to Princetown on 3 March 1956; but students of railway history and others will no doubt be able to follow the course of the line for years to come.

The remainder of Sir Thomas Tyrwhitt's railway (or tramway more strictly, since it was operated by horses) can be traced along the hillsides and through the woods above the Plym valley, winding down to the water's edge at Crabtree, near Plymouth. The visitor, armed with the $2\frac{1}{2}$-inch maps, will find the tracing of this railway a fascinating day's work.

The prison was reopened as a convict settlement in 1850 and has been much enlarged since that date. It has been decided that the prison should be progressively demolished, though the removal of this blot on the National Park will take some years to accomplish. The grim settlement of Princetown has also grown, and makes a good centre for the exploration of the western side of the Moor. In the later decades of the nineteenth century Dartmoor began to attract visitors in small numbers. By the 1870s the pleasant little town of Chagford had become 'a place of considerable resort' in the summer—so says Murray's admirable *Handbook of Devon* (1879 edition)—but Widecombe in the Moor had yet to be discovered, and is written off in the same guide-book as 'a very poor village [on] the frontier of cultivation'. The rapid development of road transport since the end of the First World War has, however, altered the scene considerably. In the summer months, convoys of elephantine motor coaches crawl up the moorland approaches and speed over the upland roads, and the greatest care is needed in coming to the Moor. But the pedestrian can quickly leave behind all evidence of the modern world. The motorist, too, is well advised to leave his car in some convenient place by the roadside and to walk to some chosen spot if he wishes to see Dartmoor as it really is and to enjoy its great solitudes. The special gazetteer of prehistoric antiquities (see pp. 23–25) is designed to enable him to do this; and even if he is not primarily interested in the antiquities he will penetrate to parts of the Moor he would not otherwise see.

SELECT BIBLIOGRAPHY

There is considerable literature about Dartmoor, not least on the historical aspect of the Moor. Among the older books the most valuable are:

Dartmoor Preservation Association Publications. Vol. 1 (all published). 1890. *A Short History of the Rights of Common upon the Forest of Dartmoor and the Commons of Devon.* Report by Stuart Moore to the Association. A valuable work for those who wish to study the medieval history of the Moor more deeply, with an Appendix of Documents.

CROSSING, W. *A Hundred Years on Dartmoor.* 1901. A kind of social survey in part of life on Dartmoor in the nineteenth century. Reprinted by David & Charles, 1967, with an introduction by Brian Le Messurier.

CROSSING, W. *Guide to Dartmoor.* 1909. A valuable encyclopaedia of the Moor and all its monuments. Reprinted by David & Charles, 1965. The essential companion for the serious Dartmoor walker.

CROSSING, W. *The Dartmoor Worker.* 1966. A collection of Crossing's essays in local newspapers, gathered together and introduced by Brian Le Messurier, and published by David & Charles. They cover the Edwardian period.

PAGE, J. L. W. *An Exploration of Dartmoor and its Antiquities.* 1889. Ran quickly into several editions. It purported to be a detailed guide to the Moor, but Crossing poured scorn on Page as an armchair traveller.

ROWE, S. *A Perambulation of the Ancient and Royal Forest of Dartmoor.*
First published in 1848. The third edition (1896) is a comprehensive
book about the history of the Moor and its antiquities, though some
of it needs revision in the light of later archaeological and historical
work.

Of the more modern works, the following will be found most useful:

Dartmoor: Building in the National Park. 1955. Published for the Devon
County Council by the Architectural Press, London, is an abundantly illustrated guide to the siting, design, materials and colours of
building on the Moor. It includes cautionary examples of how not
to build and much useful advice to those who wish to make their
home within the National Park.

COCKS, J. V. SOMERS. *The Dartmoor Bibliography: Non-Fiction.*
Dartmoor Preservation Association. 1972. Lists books and articles
under authors and subjects.

GILL, CRISPIN (ed.). *Dartmoor: a New Study.* David & Charles.
1970. The best modern survey by a collection of experts.

HARVEY, L. A. and ST. LEGER GORDON, D. *Dartmoor.* Published
in *The New Naturalist* Series. 1953. The standard work on the
natural history of the Moor. It also contains a certain amount of
useful historical material.

HOSKINS, W. G. *Devon.* 1954. Places Dartmoor in its historical and
prehistoric setting, and also has a section on the history of the tin
industry. Reprinted by David & Charles (1972).

ST. LEGER GORDON, D. *Under Dartmoor Hills.* 1954. A readable
account of life and farming on and around the Moor.

SAYER, SYLVIA. *The Outline of Dartmoor's Story.* 1951. A popular but
accurate account of the history and development of the Moor down
to 1950 for those who require a shorter introduction to the subject.
It is charmingly illustrated with line drawings by the author.

WORTH, R. H. *Dartmoor.* 1953. New edition published by David &
Charles (1967). Embodies a long lifetime's knowledge of Dartmoor
in almost all its aspects. It is painstaking and accurate, abundantly
illustrated with photographs, drawings and plans, and should be
possessed by all serious visitors to Dartmoor. Some of Worth's
conclusions may well be challenged by later work, but its great merit
is that it sets out the facts in detailed abundance.

5

General Information

BY J. V. ELMHIRST

MOST people who visit Dartmoor come by car,* and there are hundreds of miles of roads within the National Park where the motorist can get away from traffic jams and the tension of motorway driving conditions.

But no one can claim to know Dartmoor who sees it only from a car. So the visitor is advised to pull in at some convenient spot and explore, bearing in mind that it is an offence under the Road Traffic Act to drive a vehicle more than 15 yards from a public road.

Much of central Dartmoor is known as the Forest of Dartmoor, and is partly owned by the Duchy of Cornwall. The word forest in this context does not mean a large wood, but rather a royal hunting ground.

Around the circumference of the Forest are the commons. To all intents and purposes a common may be described as a piece of land owned by one person over which other people have certain rights. The fact that land is a common does not automatically mean that the general public have a right of access to it for walking and recreation. But under the National Parks Act there is an assumed right of access (subject to certain standards of conduct) on all land that is wholly or predominantly moor, heath or down. The public are therefore allowed to walk or ride over parts of Dartmoor where they have long been accustomed to go—over commons, uncultivated newtakes and the moorland part of the Forest.

ACCOMMODATION

Chiefly around but also in the approaching river valleys are scattered large and small hotels, guest houses and many suppliers of Bed and Breakfast. It is impracticable to detail these and members of the Automobile Association, Cyclists' Touring Club, Ramblers' Association, and Royal Automobile Club will find lists in their own handbooks. The Youth Hostels Association have three small hostels within the National Park and four larger ones not far away. The addresses of these hostels, together with those of the Area Secretaries of each of the organizations mentioned in this section, are on pages 41–43. Most local towns produce their individual guide-books which generally include advertisements of

---

* Certain railway lines shown on the maps in this Guide are now closed. These are Yelverton to Princetown, Totnes to Ashburton, Newton Abbot to Moretonhampstead, and Exeter to Okehampton and on to Tavistock.

accommodation. The best guide is the friend who has experienced and appreciated a visit. The Devon County Council publish a list of camping and caravan sites (see page 41).

MAPS

The Ordnance Survey publish a one-inch Tourist Map for DARTMOOR showing the National Park boundary. Then there are the Ordnance Survey 2½-inch sheets, which are admirable for the walker. The sheet numbers of the maps in this series, and the areas of the National Park which they cover, are shown on the map inside the front cover.

RECREATIONS

Bathing is a matter of finding the pool that suits you.

Fishing. Those who wish to fish within the National Park are advised to obtain a copy of a leaflet produced by the Devon County Council. Fishing is also available, with some restrictions for health reasons, on the reservoirs belonging to the Plymouth and Torbay Corporations, to whom application should be made.

Riding is available at some hotels and there are many riding stables. Those wishing to ride should obtain a copy of a leaflet produced by the Devon County Council.

Walking on Dartmoor. No better guidance can be given than by the following extracts from William Crossing's *Guide to Dartmoor* (obtainable from the County Library, Barley House, Exeter, or new copies from any bookseller).

'The explorer of the Moor who is a stranger to the locality will probably have read of the dangers of Dartmoor and may have formed the idea that it is a land of mists and bog.

It certainly cannot be denied that the Moor is often enveloped in a mist in the winter, but such will not be found to be frequently the case during the season usually chosen by the visitor to make acquaintance with it. But to be overtaken by the former, though sometimes proving rather awkward, is never dangerous, while the latter are only so to the rider to hounds who may be a stranger to the district.

A man overtaken by mist should, when not certain of his bearings, endeavour to find a stream, and having done so, follow it till he reaches the borders of the Moor or some road. Attempts to strike a straight course over the Moor will assuredly fail; he will only wander in a circle; but this plan of following a stream, though effective enough, leaves much to be desired. It is far better to be able to go in the direction he wishes, and this he may, of course, do if he has taken the precaution to provide himself with a pocket compass. I would strongly advise all who are unacquainted with the Moor to carry one when they penetrate into those parts of it that are far removed from the beaten tracks.'

SERVICE TRAINING AREAS

An artillery range has occupied an area near Okehampton since the 1870s but following a Government Inquiry in 1947 a large area was set aside for training exercise and artillery practice. There is also a rifle range on the southern slope of Rippon Tor with its essential notices and boundary posts. These areas are shown on the map inside the back cover.

There is local and national feeling against so large an area being excluded on so many days from use and from enjoyment by the public. The Park Committee find themselves from time to time concerned by this conflict of national needs; but they are glad to acknowledge the co-operative way in which the Service authorities try to meet their wishes. Nevertheless, the fact must be faced that whereas the northern stretches of the Moor include the wilder and more remote scenery and are eminently suitable for walking, they are too often under shot and shell to be easily available to the rambler. The boundaries of the danger areas are marked on the ground by red and white posts and notice boards. *When the red flags are flying (red lights by night) it is forbidden, and of course dangerous, to enter the areas.*

Notices are displayed at the following Post Offices giving the times and dates of firing: notices also appear in the *Western Morning News*, the *Western Times* and the *Express and Echo* (the Exeter evening newspaper) on Fridays:

Belstone	Ilsington	Sourton
Brentor	Lustleigh	South Zeal
Bovey Tracey	Lydford	Sticklepath
Bridestowe	Mary Tavy	Tavistock
Broadhempston	Moretonhampstead	Throwleigh
Buckfast	Okehampton	Walkhampton
Buckfastleigh	Peter Tavy	Widecombe in the
Chagford	Plymouth (Head P.O.)	Moor
Gidleigh	Postbridge	Yelverton
Holne	Princetown	
Horrabridge	Shaugh Prior	

The dates and times of firing can always be obtained by telephoning the nearest police station or post office. A recorded message giving the current programme can be heard by telephoning Plymouth 701924; Exeter 70164; Torquay 24592; or Okehampton 2939.

The northern area, dangerous when the red flags are flying, stretches from Belstone and Okehampton Hamlets to the Merrivale–Postbridge

main road and is shown on the map inside the back cover. While the
use by the Services of two other areas on the south-west can be a
nuisance, access to them is not otherwise impeded.

DARTMOOR LETTER BOXES

The custom of signing one's name in a visitors' book at a place far out
in the wilds of Dartmoor began in 1854 when James Perrott, a Dartmoor
guide from Chagford, left a small receptacle at Cranmere Pool in which
walkers deposited their visiting cards and signed in a visitors' book.
Later, when postcards were introduced, the custom began of leaving
cards there, ready-stamped and addressed, for the next visitor to collect
and post in an official box. The interest lay in seeing how long it took
them to reach the addressee.

Other letter box 'stations' have been established in recent years, and
each one now has a visitors' book and rubber stamp and pad in a metal
box. Cards, or letters, should be left in the book, but the rubber stamp
must not, of course, be used to frank the postage stamp. It can be
impressed elsewhere on the card or envelope.

PLATE 18. Bennetts Cross (medieval) near Warren House Inn

PLATE 19. Medieval Farmhouse at Yardworthy near Chagford

PLATE 20. Widecombe in the Moor

PLATE 21. Fingle Bridge over the Teign near Dunsford

USEFUL ADDRESSES

AUTOMOBILE ASSOCIATION
Area Secretary: Fanum House, Bedford Street, Exeter, Devon

CAMPING AND CARAVANNING
A list of camping and caravan sites is published by the Tourist Department of the Devon County Council, Bradninch Hall, Castle Street, Exeter, Devon

COUNCIL FOR THE PRESERVATION OF RURAL ENGLAND
Devon Branch
Hon. Secretary: Mr. F. W. Small, Nethway Cottage, Kingswear, Devon, TQ6 OEE

COUNTRYSIDE COMMISSION
1 Cambridge Gate, Regent's Park, London, N.W.1

CYCLISTS' TOURING CLUB
Devon Secretary: Mr. C. Brierly, 24 Great Headland Crescent, Preston, Paignton, Devon

DARTMOOR COMMONERS' ASSOCIATION
Hon. Secretary: Mr. R. G. Woolcock, 1 Church Lane, Tavistock, Devon

DARTMOOR LIVESTOCK PROTECTION SOCIETY
Hon. Secretary: Mrs. J. Vinson, Crooked Meadow, Stidston Lane, South Brent, Devon

DARTMOOR NATIONAL PARK PLANNING COMMITTEE
Headquarters: County Hall, Topsham Road, Exeter, Devon
Information Office: Two Bridges, Princetown (Open from Easter to September—11 a.m. to 5 p.m. each day. No postal enquiries).
All letters, and enquiries out of season to: National Parks Office, Planning Department, Devon County Council, County Hall, Topsham Road, Exeter, Devon

DARTMOOR PRESERVATION ASSOCIATION
Hon. Secretary: Mrs. E. Gaze, 8 Baron's Road, Dousland, Yelverton, Devon, PL20 6NG

DEVON ARCHAEOLOGICAL SOCIETY
Hon. Secretary: Mr. J. Bosanko, Clystlands, Saint Luke's College, Exeter, Devon, EX1 2LU

D

DEVON BIRD-WATCHING AND PRESERVATION SOCIETY

Hon. Secretary: Mr. H. P. Sitters, Uplands, Looseleigh Lane, Crownhill, Plymouth, Devon

DEVONSHIRE ASSOCIATION

Hon. Secretary: Mr. A. F. Darvall, M.A., 7, The Close, Exeter, Devon

DEVON TRUST FOR NATURE CONSERVATION

Secretary: Mr. F. M. Thomas, 2, Pennsylvania Road, Exeter, Devon, EX4 6BQ

FORESTRY COMMISSION

South-West Conservator of Forests: Flowers Hill, Brislington, Bristol, 4

NATURE CONSERVANCY

Chief Warden, Dartmoor: Mr. E. A. Roberts, Vine Cottage, Broadhempston, Totnes, Devon

RAMBLERS' ASSOCIATION

Devon Area
Hon. Secretary: Miss H. N. Biscoe, St. Morvah, Throwleigh, Okehampton, Devon

ROYAL AUTOMOBILE CLUB

Area Secretary: Princess House, 1 High Street, Exeter, Devon

SERVICES

Range Liaison Officer, Devon and Cornwall Training Areas, Crownhill Fort, Plymouth, Devon

YOUTH HOSTELS ASSOCIATION

South-West Regional Office
Secretary: Mr. Kenneth W. Tyler, Belmont House, Devonport Road, Stoke, Plymouth, Devon

Hostels in or near the National Park

(Write to the Warden, the Youth Hostel:)

Abbotsfield Hall, Tavistock, Devon (G.R.* 469737)

Belmont House, Devonport Road, Stoke, Devonport, Plymouth (G.R. 461556)

*Grid Reference

Lownard, Dartington, Totnes, Devon (G.R. 782622)
Bellever, Postbridge, Yelverton, Devon (G.R. 653773)
Castle Farm, Gidleigh, Chagford, Devon (G.R. 670884)
Steps Bridge, Dunsford, near Exeter (G.R. 803881)
Mount Wear House, Countess Wear, Exeter (G.R. 942897)

6

Two Walks across Dartmoor

BY ERIC HEMERY

ROUTE I. GIDLEIGH TO CRANMERE AND BACK

Out: 6 miles; *Return*: 7 miles

TAKE the road past Berrydown Farm ending at a wooden fence by the entrance to Scorhill House, ¼ mile south-west. Pass through a gate in the fence into Berrydown Stroll, a wide strip of land leading between new-take walls to the open Moor.

Emerging from the Stroll on to the Moor, take the path climbing Scorhill, ahead. From the summit is a fine panorama, east, of the Gidleigh and Throwleigh border-country, and ahead, of high Dartmoor. In the middle distance are large tracts of mire, and threading through them two converging streams—North Teign river and Walla Brook—toward which the Scorhill path now descends. On the slope, right of the path, is a hut circle, and below it a fine monument of the Bronze Age—Scorhill stone circle. Below this the Gidleigh leat curls round the hill, and is crossed by the Scorhill path a short way above Walla Brook Ford.

Cross Walla Brook by a single-span clapper bridge (another spans the Teign near by), turn right from the track connecting both fords, and cross the flats. (If path miry, take a parallel one left.) Cross Little Hill—an apt name—and descend to a ford in a shallow valley; cross immediately above the ford, which is disused and miry. Now make directly for Watern Tor; the climb is long, but the ground good. As you climb, a peat-cutter's shelter lies 200 yards left.

The northernmost pile of Watern Tor, from its unusual 'holed' aspect, is named Thirlestone. From here, the view of East Devon is striking. South-west, at nearly 2,000 feet, rises the huge bulk of Hanging-stone Hill—with a logan, or hanging-stone, on its western slope—and in the great mire at its eastern foot, in Watern Combe, rises Walla Brook. Descend, cross the brook below the mire, and follow a green path upward to Bow Combe Hill. Here a path runs along the col between Hangingstone and Wild Tor; follow it left.

From the summit there are magnificent views of northern Dartmoor's chief heights, including the massive Fur Tor. Now walk on a line towards the southern slope of Black Ridge (a rounded, serrated crest

44

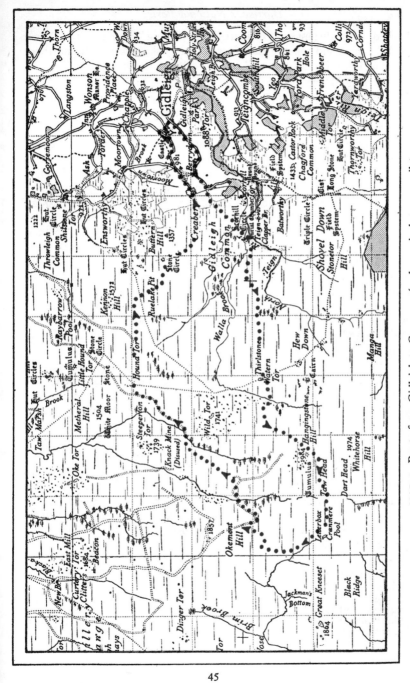

MAP 3. Route from Gidleigh to Cranmere (scale one inch to one mile).

backed by the distant cone of Hare Tor); passing Taw Head (right) bear slightly right and top the rise ahead, then make towards the northern slope of Black Ridge; this will lead directly to Cranmere.

Warning: Hangingstone marks the eastern limit of the Northern Morass and, if cloud-capped, Cranmere should not be attempted from it. Furthermore, this stretch necessitates much jumping, and is risky after heavy rains.

Cranmere has no pool and is the source of no river. Its peaty puddles, however, drain into West Okement Head, 20 yards north. Follow this infant stream to $\frac{1}{4}$ mile below its first fall.* Fine views lie ahead of Dartmoor's highest ground, High Willhays and Yes Tor, both over 2,000 feet. Make for a large peat chasm; this is an artificial cut through the peat to provide a safe passage for horsemen.† Pass through it to a wide clearing known as Huggaton Court. Here, near a large peat-pool, sometimes dry in summer, begins a track leading to the military road; reaching this latter, turn sharp right, cross the Taw at a paved ford, and climb to a splinter-proof hut on Ockside Hill. Strike across the hill's eastern flank on a line to Hound Tor; at the north-eastern foot of Ockside follow a path to a picturesque ford on the Steeperton Brook. A few yards downstream (left bank) is a tinner's house. Cross the brook and walk to Hound Tor; on the way, notice how effectively the Belstone range is framed by Metheral Hole (left).

From Hound Tor (which gives a fine view of High Willhays, and Steeperton Tor rising from the head of Taw Marsh), walk due east to the south-western foot of Kennon Hill. Here is a prehistoric village, as yet unsurveyed, which includes pound, hut circles, and possible kist-vaens grouped lower down the hill, right. Continue to south-eastern foot of Kennon, near which is an unrestored monument, Buttern stone circle.

Follow a track, right, curving round the southern foot of Buttern Hill, noticing a hut circle, right, and enter Creaber Stroll. Below is a disused gateway, once part of Creaber Pound; into this, during the great pony drifts of former years, the animals were driven. Now take the Moortown road, turning right at Old Rectory Cross. Gidleigh lies $\frac{1}{2}$ mile down the lane.

---

*The return route given here is bog-free, and practicable both for walkers and for riders.

†Such passes on Dartmoor arise not from military activity, but from the enterprise and teamwork of the late Frank Phillpotts and the moormen. See 'The Phillpotts peat passes of northern Dartmoor' by Brian Le Messurier, *Transactions of the Devonshire Association*, 1965.

ROUTE II. PRINCETOWN TO CORNWOOD

13 *miles*

Walk up Plymouth Hill, and take to the common, left, immediately beyond the two Duchy cottages. Walk on a line to Peek Hill (south-west). From the crest of the common* the Meavy valley is visible, flanked by some fine tors, particularly Leather and Sheeps Tors. The beautiful little Harter Tor is next ahead, in approaching which veer slightly right to visit some hut circles, attractively sited and well preserved. Now cross a small depression and ascend to Harter Tor, its characteristic lines silhouetted to advantage ahead: from its summit, a further stretch of the Meavy opens out, beneath Black Tor, opposite.

Slightly west of south from Harter Tor, a large cairn crests the saddle between Cramber Tor and Raddick Hill. By making for this, the Harter Brook, left, will be crossed below its head mire, and an ancient track struck as it comes up from Black Tor and Harter Fords, right. Follow the track past the cairn, over the saddle, and across the Devonport Leat (cut in 1793–96) by a partly fallen clapper bridge, to a point immediately beyond a deep gully some 200 yards south-east of the leat. From here, another valley opens out ahead—that of the Newleycombe Lake—bounded by the bold Combeshead and Down Tors. Right, the fine tors first seen from the common near Princetown provide a mountainous background to a large and beautiful lake; this is Burrator reservoir, formed in 1898 by the damming of the Meavy to provide a water supply for Plymouth. Below the tors, and almost surrounding the lake, is a large conifer plantation. The entire scene, sweeping from the lonely heights of the Southern Marsh, east, to the gleaming lake and colourful tors, west, is exceptionally beautiful.

Near by (left) are some mounds, and beyond them, a granite cross. Near the mounds is a huge, water-filled hole known as Clasiwell (Crazywell, Classenwell) Pool, the remains of an old mine working. Sunlight gives it charm, but lying grey and still beneath a mist, it can be forbidding. The cross is finely shaped; formerly, it probably stood a little south of its present situation, marking a medieval trackway over the Moor.†

Below the cross is a gert, or gully, where once the tinner dug for his ore; follow this, cross a wide, gravelly track, and descend towards Newleycombe Lake on a line to Hingston Hill (the rounded crest of the col east of Down Tor). Keep above a miry bottom, right, and pass through two gateways in the outer enclosures of Clasiwell Farm, of which the ruins appear some distance right. Another—and very large—gert lies left; descend to its foot, a delightful, sheltered dell. Here, near

* Known as Middle Hill. † Another cross stands to the south-east.

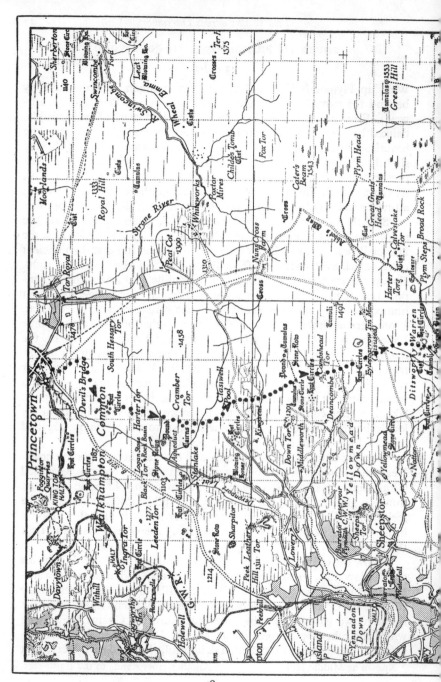

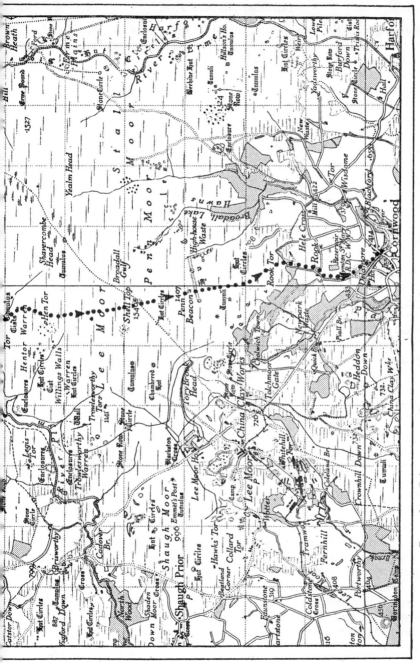

MAP 4. Route from Princetown to Cornwood (scale one inch to one mile). (See footnote page 37.)

the stream, is the course of a disused tinner's leat, crossed by a wide, single-span clapper bridge. Between leat and stream are the ruins of a building, in style and site an obvious adjunct to the old tin-streaming works in this lovely valley. Cross Newleycombe Lake behind the building and ascend Hingston Hill.

Mounting the col, a striking view presents itself of Combeshead Tor, jagged against the skyline, seen through the boldly erect stones of a splendid Bronze Age monument; this consists of a well-preserved stone row and retaining circle, the latter enclosing a ruined grave.

Now go directly to Combeshead Tor—a massive core and clitter. From here is the first unbroken view of the great ridge south of the Plym, rising from Trowlesworthy Tors, right, to Langcombe Head, left. Beyond the point of its fall to Trowlesworthy, a white conical peak denotes the Lee Moor china clay works. Below, and north of the ridge, appears the dark mass of Hen Tor.

From Combeshead Tor, cross the Combeshead Brook below its head mire, left. Walk round the head of a small, miry combe, right, in which rises a feeder of the Deancombe Brook, and make for the saddle in a ridge immediately south, keeping a Plymouth Corporation Waterworks boundary stone left. Crossing the saddle will lead to the Eylesboro mine road and provide a fine view of the Plym country; right is the noble bulk of Sheeps Tor, an eminence so far conspicuous throughout this route; monopolizing the prospect left is the high and stony hill of Eylesboro, and on its slopes the relics of a large tin mine; south of Eylesboro are the rocks of another Harter Tor—being the higher of two overlooking the Plym's right bank; beyond Eylesboro lies the high and lonely plateau of the Southern Marsh.

Directly ahead is a small valley with the musical name of Thrushel* Combe, through which flows a tiny feeder of the Plym. Above the brook's right bank is an eighteenth-century tin-smelting house, the last to work on Dartmoor; with its granite flue, possible coal-fired furnace, and pit for a 16-foot water-wheel, it marks the transition between the earlier blowing-houses and the large mines of the Industrial Revolution.

Cross Thrushel Combe Brook at a ford below the mine, and walk along the left bank. Follow a disused leat veering left, which will lead to a well-preserved kistvaen (right of the leat), the remains of the barrow formerly enclosing it being conspicuous.

This ancient grave marks the threshold of the finest group of sepulchral monuments on Dartmoor—the ' Drizzlecombe ' menhirs and stone rows. Looking south from the kistvaen, down into the Plym valley, three huge menhirs rise from the turf, each the terminal of a stone row

*Locally pronounced 'Drishel'—interpreted by Ordnance Survey as 'Drizzle'.

leading from a ruined cairn-covered grave. The greatest of these menhirs is 14 feet in height, and has a remarkably shaped head. Walking towards it from the kistvaen, two pounds appear above (left), enclosing the hut circles in which the monument builders probably once lived.

Now make for the Plym, which in normal flow may conveniently be crossed near a mountain-ash tree—picturesquely rooted in a tiny island, mid-stream. At the foot of the opposite hill is a large hollow, and in it the remains of an early tinner's mill; here are still to be seen the original mortar stones on which the tin ore was crushed. From Cole's Mill, as this little ruin is known, ascend the steep bank of the hollow, when a narrow valley will come into view, south. This is Shavercombe, and on the further hillside above it are the tiny Shavercombe Tor, and a pre-historic pound.

Descend towards Shavercombe, crossing a gully known as Watern Combe, and keeping below a small mire, left. Cross Shavercombe Brook and ascend via the pound to the tor. From here is a pleasing view of the Plym downstream, the old Ditsworthy Warren House nestling on its northern bank. From the tor, return to the combe, but at a point upstream where some tree-tops protrude above its western bank. Here is a scene of unusual charm: a miniature canyon, and a waterfall with a deep, dark pool at its foot, overhung by rowan, sycamore, willow, hawthorn and oak. This delectable spot is known as Shavercombe Fall.

Some way above the combe, south, and below a rock-clitter, is a mound topped by a leaning slab; here, within the opened cairn, is a fine kistvaen. From here make directly for Hen Tor. Behind this mass are two subsidiary piles, concealed from the north but now visible—one being admittedly like a sitting hen!* It is worth while climbing the main mass to survey the panorama below and beyond. The entire moorland course of the Plym can be traced, from Great Gnat's Head, east, to the gorge below Dewerstone, west. Beyond lies the beautiful country crossed in the early part of this route, and backed by the bulky North Hessary Tor, with the B.B.C. television mast on its summit, and Princetown church at its foot.

Turning south, and passing a bond stone of the old Hen Tor Warren, left, make for a saddle in the great ridge above. The entire summit of this huge, whale-backed ridge is a featureless, wind-swept wilderness, and if mist is likely it is best avoided. In summer, east of the saddle, are great carpets of golden asphodel and snowy cotton-grass, where firm ground surrenders to a sea of marsh.

South of the saddle, still higher land lies ahead, crowned by a square-shaped rock-pile; this is the lofty Shell Top. On a clear day the view

* But name derivation is a hazardous pursuit on Dartmoor!

from here is most impressive—particularly seawards. The gleaming finger of the Plym estuary leads into a wide stretch of the English Channel; east rise the high hills above Erme and Yealm valleys; below, a mile south, is the fine frontier height of Penn Beacon, connected with Shell Top by a reave.

Walk to Penn Beacon, which affords a detailed prospect of the luxuriant border-country and South Hams beyond: Hanger Down, an offshoot of the Moor crowned by a conspicuous round plantation, flanks the Yealm valley, east, whilst above the river's western bank is Cornwood, the soft grey of church and cottages melting into the richer hue of the wooded country surrounding it.

Descend from Penn Beacon to the rocky spur of the common below, known as Rook Tor. Here, beside a track leading to West Rook Gate, is the segment of a large hut circle, despoiled, no doubt, by the builder of the ancient wall bounding Rook Wood, below.

Pass through the gate and down the lane, leaving Middle Rook, left, and West Rook, right. Beyond a second and ruined gateway—obviously once of fine proportions—an avenue leads across Heathfield Down to Delamore House; take a grassy track, left, leading to Cornwood, and joining the Meavy road just below the village.* The fine and spacious old church of Cornwood is dedicated, like that of Princetown, to St. Michael and all his Angels—a fitting touch at the beginning and end of this beautiful walk.

---

*From here, a bus service connects with Plymouth. The railway station, on the main Exeter–Totnes–Plymouth line, has been closed.

7

Places of special interest in the National Park

BY W. G. HOSKINS

THE brief notes which follow give only an outline of the interesting places within the National Park. Visitors who wish to be more fully informed about particular matters or places are referred to the bibliographies at the end of each chapter of this Guide.

A word of caution is necessary here about access to houses mentioned in these notes, most of which are actively working farmsteads. Farming is a business like any other, and the visitor will bear in mind that some times of the day are more convenient for a visit than others. Again, these farmhouses and the cultivated land around them (including the grass-land) are *private property*, to which the ordinary rules of social intercourse apply no less than in the towns. This is especially true as regards the careful shutting of gates wherever one goes.

The Devonshire farmer and his wife are naturally hospitable and welcome the considerate visitor who takes an intelligent interest in their house and its history; but the inconsiderate visitor is a plague to all around him and discourages everyone.

ABBOTS WAY is the name given to an ancient trackway across the southern part of the Moor. There is no authority for the belief that it connected the abbeys of Buckland and Buckfast, although one can piece together a route between the two places with some ingenuity. The name arose comparatively late and is of no historical significance: merely further evidence of the obsession with monks, nuns, underground passages and priests' hiding-holes that bedevils so much topographical writing and occasionally finds its way on to the map. Nevertheless, the trackway is of considerable age, most probably early medieval, and must have been a recognized way over the southern part of the Moor from the Plym valley to the Dart. It now offers one of the most solitary and satisfying walks on the Moor, far from any of the summer crowds and the motor coaches. The line of the track is clearly marked on the one-inch map, but the $2\frac{1}{2}$-inch map is a better guide. At Redlake it crosses the southern blanket bog. The construction of the new Avon Dam below Dean Moor does not break the line of the Abbots Way, though it may diminish its solitude a little.

ASHBURTON, small and quiet, is now by-passed by the busy Exeter-Plymouth main road, at the terminus of one of the most picturesque branch railways in England, running down to Totnes.* It is a convenient tourist centre for exploring the south-eastern side of the National Park, and has a few architectural attractions of its own. The slate-hung houses are a feature of South Devon towns, many of them dating from the late sixteenth to the eighteenth centuries. The early nineteenth-century Market House is also worth noticing. The parish church, with its handsome granite tower, has some notable things, but also lost much at the 'restoration' by G. E. Street, including a fine rood-screen which was replaced by the present poor structure. Ashburton was formerly a stannary town, a cloth-manufacturing town, and a lively coaching place full of inns; now it is a quiet residential town living on its history.

BELSTONE village has lost its original moorland appearance, having been 'discovered' some sixty years ago with some disastrous effects on its building. The little granite church has been restored in a painful fashion, but retains some light sweet bells. There is, however, some striking moorland scenery in the parish, notably Belstone Cleave through which the infant Taw dashes along; and a fairly easy walk takes one up to the summit of Cawsand Beacon† from which on a good day there are sweeping views of cultivated Devon to the north and of the wildest part of the Moor to the south. Cawsand was an important link in the great chain of beacons which operated above all during the sixteenth century.

BRENTOR, on the extreme western edge of the National Park, is an isolated hill—actually a volcanic cone and not a granite tor at all—rising to 1,130 feet and forming an unmistakable landmark for many miles around (Plate 23). From the summit, on which stands the little church of St. Michael, wonderful views of western Devon and eastern Cornwall are to be had. The church, built here about 1140–50, has been little altered since then and is well worth the scramble up the steep slopes strewn with volcanic debris. Around the base of the hill runs an earthwork of unknown purpose. It is possible that the hill was a site with some religious significance long before the first Christian church was built here: for wherever one goes on this side of Devon the eye is irresistibly drawn to this cone of black rock rising out of the sea of grassland.

BRIDFORD lies 700 feet up in the eastern foothills of the Moor, which harbour barytes mines and disused lead mines. Bridford Bridge, the

---

* This line was closed to passenger traffic in 1958.

† The name 'Cawsand' was unknown before the nineteenth century. The true name from time immemorial was Cosdon, pronounced locally as *Cossen*.

most interesting bridge over the Teign, was built about 1500 and widened in the nineteenth century. The village contains several good moorstone houses. The granite church is notable for its ancient fittings (glass, stalls, bench-ends, pulpit and wagon roofs), and above all for a richly carved rood-screen, *c.* 1530 in date. The parish contains much beautiful hill and woodland scenery (note Bridford Wood above the Teign), rising to over 1,100 feet in places. Blackingstone Rock and Heltor Rock are fine viewpoints. Particularly interesting farmhouses are Laployd Barton, Weeke Barton, Woodlands and Burnicombe. The country is interesting here for the occasional patches of limestone rock, where the pale toadflax may sometimes be found in the hedgerows.

BUCKFASTLEIGH, now a small market town of little interest in itself, is chiefly notable for the rebuilt Buckfast Abbey, about one mile to the north. The abbey was originally founded about 1030, and re-founded by monks from Savigny in 1134–36. It became a Cistercian house a few years later (1148) and so remained until its dissolution in 1539. The site passed into lay hands for more than three centuries, but in 1882 was acquired by a community of French Benedictines. In 1907 the rebuilding of the abbey church was begun, and was completed in 1932 when the church was consecrated by Cardinal Bourne amid solemn rejoicing. The abbey church follows the foundations of the former church and is mainly in the style transitional between Norman and Early English. The general character, says Pevsner, is French and Cistercian, with the exception of the tower over the crossing (completed in 1938). The abbey is a place of considerable resort during the summer months, but there are good arrangements for dealing with the traffic.

Higher Buckfast Mill, near the abbey, is a remarkable industrial building of about 1800, when Buckfastleigh was one of the principal woollen towns of Devon.

The parish extends westwards for miles, up to Ryder's Hill, 1,691 feet. The so-called Abbots Way (q.v.) begins in the parish, near Cross Furzes, and makes a splendid moorland walk across the wild southern hills which are comparatively little known.

BUCKLAND IN THE MOOR is everything that the visitor expects in Devon, but often in vain. With its moorstone cottages and thatched roofs set among beech trees and a luxuriant green vegetation, it is one of the show villages of the county and yet remains quite unspoilt, thanks to benevolent and intelligent planning by a private landowner. The moor-stone church is wholly delightful, a characteristic little Devon church in appearance mostly late fifteenth or early sixteenth century but offering much work of an earlier period to those who have eyes to see. The rood-screen is notably good, and its paintings better in quality than most in Devon where the screen-paintings are not generally of much artistic merit. The church contains also some pleasant eighteenth-century furniture. Cockingford Mill on the Widecombe road is worth seeing. The wooded slopes of the Webburn valley with Holne Chase rising on the opposite side of the gorge should be explored on foot: there are excellent paths for this purpose.

CHAGFORD was one of the earliest centres for the exploration of Dartmoor when the tourist industry began nearly a century ago, and it is still the best centre for exploring the eastern side of the National Park. The large parish is almost everywhere romantically beautiful, from the ever-lovely Teign valley to the high moorlands of its western and southern fringes. The lower ground of the parish is a network of narrow winding lanes, of Saxon and early medieval origin, in which much caution is necessary in the holiday months. Scattered about these lanes are a score of old farmhouses of the characteristic Dartmoor type. Particularly interesting are Hole, Yeo, and Yardworthy (where there are remains of a medieval farmhouse in the farmyard, Plate 19), Rushford Barton, Collihole, and Whiddon Park. Like a number of small towns around the moorland edge, Chagford was formerly deeply interested in tin-mining and cloth-working, but all this industrial activity vanished long ago. There is much good small-town building. Notice especially the sixteenth-century granite house on the south side of the church yard (formerly the Church House) and the Three Crowns Inn of the same period. The church is a fine example of granite ashlar building, with a notable Elizabethan tomb of Sir John Whiddon (1575). Stiniel (or Stinhall), 1½ miles south of the town, is worth visiting as an almost untouched specimen of a Dartmoor farmhouse of the time of Elizabeth I.

CHRISTOW, on the eastern edge of the National Park, is a hilly parish with much semi-moorland scenery, falling away to the Teign valley. In the west of the parish the reservoirs of the South-West Devon Water Board, with the woods that almost surround them, make a delightful drive or walk. The parish church has one of the finest granite towers in Devon. Internally the fittings are of considerable interest: carved bench-ends, a coloured rood-screen, and a Norman font. Canonteign House, the seat of Viscount Exmouth, replaced an older manor-house about 1820. Old Canonteign is a Tudor house, now in a state of pleasing decay beside an abandoned lead-mine.

CORNWOOD is a large parish at the south-western corner of the National Park with many beautiful walks. These provide excellent examples of

PLATE 22. Clapper bridge over River Cowsic

PLATE 23. Brentor and its medieval church

PLATE 24. Strip-lynchets of Saxon and medieval origin above Challacombe

PLATE 25. Ash-house at West Combe farm, North Bovey

the rugged, boulder-strewn woods of the steep-sided valleys on the margins of the Moor. The moorland above here is one of the most thickly-studded parts of Dartmoor for antiquities of all kinds—Bronze Age hut circles and stone rows, and smelting-houses of medieval and later tinners. Scattered about the parish are a great number of moorland farmhouses of some age. Cholwich Town (*c.* 1500) has the remains of an even earlier farmstead in the yard (possibly thirteenth century). Hanger, Stert, Wisdome, and Higher Hele are mostly houses built about 1600, the last being the ancestral house of the well-known Hele family. Blachford and Slade are mansions of considerable architectural interest; and Fardel (which like Slade lies just outside the Park) is most attractive of all. It is substantially a small medieval manor-house and it retains a perfect example of a private chapel, built in 1432. The manor belonged to Sir Walter Raleigh's family for several generations.

Lee Moor and Shaugh Moor china clay works lie mainly outside the Park boundaries, and are worth seeing as a piece of industrial landscape.

CRANMERE POOL is one of the loneliest parts of the northern Moor. It lies very near both Taw Head and Dart Head, where the two principal rivers of Dartmoor rise. Those who like to trace the beginnings of rivers will find this a very rewarding little area, for the Teign, Okement and Tavy also rise not far away. This area is indeed one of the two extensive blanket bogs of Dartmoor which act as gigantic sponges and give rise to most of the inland water of Devon. It is therefore an area of vital importance to the whole county: Dartmoor is the Great Source. A military road now runs almost up to Cranmere and much of its former glamour is gone, but walkers from any other direction must be prepared for a very exhausting day's toil. Such a walk should not be undertaken after a spell of wet weather, or without the aid of the 2½-inch map. None of the Dartmoor bogs is dangerous, but one may have some unpleasant experiences in bad weather.*

DARTMEET, where the East and West Dart join forces, is deservedly one of the most popular places within the National Park. Above it lies the open moorland, and below the river enters an almost gorge-like valley, densely wooded on both sides and romantically beautiful even for Devon. It is not followed by any road, but footpaths enable one to see some of this spectacular scenery at close range. Other excellent walks are up the valley to Babeny and beyond, westwards to Huccaby and Hexworthy, or southwards to the reservoir on Holne Moor. The moor-

* For Cranmere see also page 46. Though there is no pool today, there must have been one originally for the name means " Crow's mere, or pool "

E

land round about is thickly strewn with hut circles and other remains of the Bronze Age.

DEAN PRIOR is notable for its association with Robert Herrick, who was vicar here from 1629 to 1674, except for the years between 1647 and 1662 when he was ejected by the Commonwealth authorities. He disliked Dean and Devonshire very much, but he died here all the same and is buried in the churchyard in an unmarked grave. The vicarage contains a good deal of Herrick's original house at the back of a more modern building. Westwards the parish rises to high open moorland, where it is traversed by the so-called Abbots Way (q.v.).

DREWSTEIGNTON is one of the most varied and beautiful areas within the National Park, with deeply rolling country broken by small combes and above all by the luxuriantly wooded gorge of the Teign. Fingle Bridge (q.v.) is in this parish and is the most notable of all the Dartmoor bridges for the beauty of its setting. The Iron Age hill-fort of Preston-bury Castle, high above the bridge, commands a superb view and is far less frequented.

At Shilstone, two miles west of the village, is the so-called Spinster's Rock, the internal structure of a megalithic tomb of late Neolithic date (Plate 9).

The village centre is most pleasing, with its moorstone (granite) houses covered with thatch, and its attractive parish church. Most notable of the secular buildings is the Church House which was left to the parish in 1546. This is an excellent example of moorland building in the early Tudor period. These Church Houses, of which there are several good specimens within the National Park, served the purpose in former times of village halls; some are still used for this purpose.

About one mile south-west of the church is Castle Drogo, superbly sited on a promontory dominating the Teign valley. This granite building is one of Sir Edwin Lutyens' masterpieces (1911-30) and is the last country house to be built in England. The house is not shown to the public, but good views of it are obtained from round about. Among the many interesting farmhouses of the parish, Preston, Shilstone and Drascombe should be seen.

DUNSFORD was one of the more unspoiled villages of Devon with a good deal of whitewashed cob and granite building dominated by the parish church, but has been degraded in recent years by the addition of speculative building unrelated to the traditional character of the village. The church was rather too thoroughly restored but contains pleasant woodwork of seventeenth- and eighteenth-century date, and monuments to the Fulfords. Great Fulford (just outside the Park) has been the home of the Fulfords since at least the twelfth century. They still flourish here but the interesting house (mainly a Tudor quadrangular building in a pleasant park) is not normally shown to the public.

The parish is especially notable for its natural scenery, above all along the Teign valley. Steps Bridge and Clifford Bridge are good starting points for exploring the valley bottom on foot (see Fingle Bridge below). The weir at Steps Bridge offers rich opportunities for studying the aquatic insects of the river. Wild daffodils and occasionally clumps of snowdrops make the Teign valley delightful in the spring.

FINGLE BRIDGE over the Teign is a well-known 'beauty spot' even in Devon, and is best avoided in the height of the holiday season when large coaches fill the approach roads. It is built of granite and is probably of sixteenth-century date (Plate 21). On the hilltops above are the impressive Iron Age fortresses of Prestonbury Castle and Cranbrook Castle, constructed to hold in check the aboriginal inhabitants of Dartmoor in the generations immediately preceding the Roman conquest.

The walk down the Teign from Fingle, past Clifford Bridge to Steps Bridge, offers almost a cross-section of Dartmoor woodlands, from oak standards, through coppice both maintained and neglected, to the more modern conifer plantations, either in pure stands or intermixed with other species.

GIDLEIGH is a good moorland village, hardly more than a hamlet. The parish church is a simple granite building of early sixteenth-century date. Near it are the remains of the so-called Gidleigh Castle, which was in reality a fortified manor-house, probably built about 1300. It is a small keep-like structure with a cellar below and a solar (or living-room) above. The natural scenery of the parish is perhaps the chief attraction, with its rocky combes, cascading streams, boulder-strewn fields rising to open moorland, the usual Bronze Age antiquities (chiefly the hut circles on Buttern Hill), and massive old farmsteads along the lanes.

HARFORD is the gateway to a beautiful part of the National Park—the upper valley of the Erme. Here is the richest concentration of Bronze Age remains on the whole Moor, and also numerous remains of medieval and later tinners. The $2\frac{1}{2}$-inch maps are necessary for the proper exploration of this fascinating piece of country. A mile or so up the Erme valley is Piles Copse, one of the three dwarf-oak woods of Dartmoor. The small granite church beside the Erme is attractive in the moorland fashion. Notice the inscription on the chancel roof commemorating Walter Hele, parson in 1539. The altar tomb has two brasses, one to Thomas Williams (Speaker of the House of Commons, 1563), and the other to the parents of John Prideaux, Bishop of Worcester. At Hall, half a mile west of the church, was born Elizabeth Chudleigh, the notorious Duchess of Kingston (1720–88).

HENNOCK lies high in the wildish country between the Teign and Bovey valleys, with much fine scenery—wooded combes, the reservoirs at the north-west end of the parish, and impressive views of the eastern edge of Dartmoor from the high road that runs westward out of the village. The parish church is pleasing though somewhat over-restored, but the fifteenth-century rood-screen retains some of its ancient paintings of saints. Notice too the enriched canopy of honour above the screen, a feature in many Devonshire churches so often missed by the visitor. One should never fail to raise one's eyes in churches in this part of England. There are the usual interesting farmhouses in the parish of which the best are perhaps Warmhill, Longlands (in the village), and Higher Crockham.

HOLNE lies high above the west bank of the Dart, which is here thickly wooded along both banks, notably at Holne Wood and Holne Chase. Westwards the parish rises to over 1,500 feet, and there is a fine walk along the so-called Sandy Way to the source of the Avon. The reservoir on Holne Moor should also be visited. It shows how difficult it is to make a reservoir look natural. Both Holne Bridge and New Bridge, carrying the main Ashburton–Two Bridges road over the Dart, are picturesque medieval bridges. Great care is needed in negotiating both. Holne church is a building of about 1300, enlarged about 1500. The fine screen, with much good detail, and the carved pulpit date from the late medieval enlargement. The vicarage, an attractive late Georgian building, was the birthplace of Charles Kingsley (June 12, 1819), while his father was curate-in-charge here.

HORRABRIDGE takes its name from the ancient bridge over the River Walkham: it is certainly the oldest bridge in this part of Devon and may be round about 1500 in date. The walks around Horrabridge are full of magnificent views and strikingly beautiful river scenery, especially perhaps at Double Waters, where the Walkham and the Tavy meet. This may be reached by a walk of between two and three miles by footpaths over Roborough Down. There is good walking also along the lanes following the Walkham valley upwards towards Woodtown.

ILSINGTON parish takes in three of the most well-known Dartmoor tors—Rippon Tor (1,563 feet), Saddle Tor (1,380 feet), and Haytor (1,490 feet). The last-named is easily accessible by car (Plate 1) and affords superb views of the coastline, the Teign estuary, and the rich, cultivated lowlands of Devon to the eastward with the Haldon ridge in the background. There are extensive granite quarries near by. The Haytor Granite Railway, opened in 1820 and operated by horses, was the earliest railway in Devon. The 'rails' were of granite setts, and the track is still partly visible (see page 70). Ilsington church is of the usual moorland type, with a particularly rich rood-screen. At Bagtor, John Ford, the dramatist, was born in 1586, his father then being squire of Ilsington. Other places worth seeing in the parish are Bagtor Mill, Colesworthy, and Ingsdon Mills.

LUSTLEIGH village contains much good moorland building, notably the Cleave Hotel and the house beside it, and some cottages to the south-east of the church. Outside the village, the old manor-house at Mapstone is mainly a medieval house with an open-roofed hall. The oldest part of the house is fourteenth century in date. Foxworthy and Foxworthy Mill, South Harton, and Caseley are all good seventeenth-century farmhouses of a characteristic local type. South Harton has some fine granite barns. Waye and Higher Hisley are also noteworthy. The parish church is an attractive and interesting building, of thirteenth- and sixteenth-century date, with a rare type of screen which is said to date from the reign of Mary (1553–58). In the west of the parish the scenery of Lustleigh Cleave above the Bovey river is locally famous.

Near Lustleigh is the hamlet of Wrayland, where the Hall or Court House is a notable but much restored house of the local type. Good houses on this side of the river are Forder, Kelly, and Knowle.

LYDFORD is now a rather nondescript village but was in Anglo-Saxon times a fortified borough with a mint. The original earthen rampart that defended the borough may still be seen as one comes along the main road into the village from the north-east. The remarkable Lydford Gorge, 70 feet deep, is now National Trust property and may be entered at Lydford Bridge for a walk down-river through the wooded glen upon payment of a small fee.

In the village itself the most notable feature is the so-called castle, a great square stone keep built in the year 1195 as a prison for offenders against the special laws of the forest and the stannaries. The tinners had their own statutes and courts, and it was alleged often threw men into Lydford Castle without the formality of a trial. The parish church near by is a fifteenth-century granite building for the most part, with some excellent modern woodwork (especially the rood-screen and the carved bench-ends). In the churchyard is the curious and often-quoted epitaph to George Routleigh, a local watchmaker.

E*

The parish of Lydford technically extends over the greater part of Dartmoor, including Princetown, but the principal places in the parish are dealt with under separate heads in the gazetteer.

MANATON is a good moorland village, with a typical fifteenth-century church notable for its rood-screen which extends right across the church. About a mile south-east of the village are the Becka Falls on the stream of the same name, well worth a special visit after heavy rain. At other times the falls are a disappointing trickle. The parish extends far westwards into the Moor and includes the outstanding prehistoric monument of Grimspound (see page 20). At Neadon is a barn, formerly a fifteenth-century house, with the dwelling-house on the first floor and a cattle-byre beneath. So far this remains a unique type. Other places to visit in the parish are Foxworthy Bridge and Ford Farm, which is Tudor or earlier. The farm buildings are exceptionally interesting and include the finest ash-house in the county, and some ancient pig-sties. Great Houndtor is another good farmhouse with stone barns. Between Hound Tor and Great Tor a deserted medieval village was discovered (see page 32) a few years ago and has since been scientifically excavated.

MARY TAVY lies on the western side of the National Park. Its high ground (e.g. Gibbet Hill, 1,158 feet) commands fine views of the Cornish moors and hills. There are a number of abandoned copper and tin mines in the parish, notably the Devon Friendship Mine near the village and Wheal Betsy near Gibbet Hill. Among the interesting farmhouses are North Warne and Wringworthy. The parish church is pleasant, but was too drastically restored in the 1870s.

MEAVY takes its name from the river here, an ancient British name meaning 'merry brook'. Wigford Down is dotted with a number of prehistoric remains (hut circles, etc.) but the parish is perhaps chiefly notable for the earliest specific reference to tin-working on Dartmoor—at the hamlet of Brisworthy in 1168. Brisworthy lies very near the upper Plym, one of the richest areas on the Moor for evidences of the Bronze Age. Meavy church is of some interest, the chancel arch showing some traces of an early Norman building, though the greater part of the church was rebuilt in the early sixteenth century. Marchants Cross, about half a mile south-east of the village, is a good example of a medieval cross. The road by which it stands is of great antiquity, continuing on over Lynch Common to Cadover Bridge (over the Plym) and so over Shaugh Moor towards an unknown destination. It may possibly be a local Roman road. Goodameavy and Greenwell are interesting houses in the parish.

MORETONHAMPSTEAD is a pleasant little town on the edge of the Moor. At Mardon Down, to the north-east, the hills rise to 1,170 feet and command wide views. Cranbrook Castle and Wooston Castle, on the northern edge of the parish, are hill-forts of the early Iron Age. The former is especially impressive and was constructed mainly in the first century B.C. to command the deep gorge of the Teign. It should perhaps be explained that in Devon the word 'castle' is frequently used for a prehistoric earthwork.

In Moreton itself the parish church is chiefly notable for its commanding granite tower erected in 1418, and for a modest memorial of George Bidder (1806–78), the famous 'calculating boy' who was later associated with Robert Stephenson, the great railway engineer, and who designed the Victoria Docks, London. The town contains a good deal of building of the sixteenth to nineteenth centuries, of which the most notable are the colonnaded almshouses (dated 1637) and the White Hart Inn (early nineteenth century). Out in the parish the most interesting houses are Sloncombe, Meacombe, Combe Farm, Bowden Farm and Addiscott.

NORTH BOVEY is one of the 'show' villages of Devon, but remains unspoilt. It stands around a small green, and upon a hillside commanding views of the eastern wall of Dartmoor. The parish church is the usual Perpendicular granite structure, with carved bosses in the wagon roofs. Notice especially those in the chancel roof. Many of the cottages at the village centre are seventeenth century in date. Among the outlying farmhouses, Yard is the most interesting. The west of the parish rises to high moorland, thick with prehistoric remains, while on Headland Warren are numerous tin-works dating from medieval and Elizabethan times (see under Warren House Inn). The scenery is everywhere of great beauty. At West Combe Farm there survives one of the best specimens of an ash-house in which the wood-ash from the hearths was stored until it could be spread on the fields (Plate 25). Lettaford, about three miles west of the parish church (not far from B 3212), is a good example of a medieval Dartmoor hamlet. One farmhouse (*c.* 1600) is especially typical and attractive.

OKEHAMPTON town lies outside the National Park, but an extensive part of the rural parish is included, taking in the two highest tors on the Moor and the highest ground in England south of the Peak—High Willhays (2,038 feet) and Yes Tor (2,030 feet). Most of this upland area lies within the military firing zone and is not often accessible, but information on this score is readily obtainable in the local newspapers or at Okehampton Post Office. The climb to the summit of these tors should not be missed, especially on days of high visibility, when most of Devon and a good deal of Cornwall lies spread out below.

Okehampton Park, so called, was formerly a hunting park of the great Courtenay family, earls of Devon, but is now firmly gripped by the military. Their castle, which is just within the Park boundary but outside the military zone, occupies a commanding site above the West Okement river. The square keep probably dates from soon after 1152, when the Courtenays took up their residence in Devon (they are still here, but now at Powderham beside the Exe estuary). The other buildings within the castle precinct represent a rebuilding of about 1300, and include the remains of the great hall and buttery, and the kitchen with its two ovens, all on the north side of the bailey; and the lodge, wardrooms and chapel, on the south side. The whole site is romantically beautiful, and was the subject of a fine painting by Richard Wilson (1714–82). It was in its day the strongest castle between Exeter and Launceston.

At Meldon, about two miles to the south-west, the Southern Railway reached the highest point on its system, and crossed the West Okement by a viaduct carried 160 feet above the river. Great quarries of stone are also to be seen here used mainly for extracting railway ballast. Black Tor Beare is a striking example of the dwarfed oakwoods of Dartmoor, and the walk up the West Okement from Meldon, passing the reservoir and the Island of Rocks, is well worth attempting.

PETER TAVY is an immense parish which includes the well-known Tavy Cleave, where the infant River Tavy breaks out of the Moor. Near by, on Standon Down, is a fine example of a large unenclosed prehistoric village. This area lies within the military zone and care should be taken that no firing is about to take place. There are warning flags and other adequate notices, and visitors should not allow themselves to be deterred from visiting this interesting spot if the military are quiescent. The parish church was ruined in an abominable Victorian restoration but there are several interesting secular buildings in the village and parish. Coxtor is a good example of a moorland yeoman's dwelling in the seventeenth century. Other farmsteads worth visiting, preferably on foot, are Willsworthy, Bagga Tor (of considerable interest as an example of a peasant dwelling), Nat Tor (a frontier farmstead), and Wapsworthy.

POSTBRIDGE is a small settlement and tourist centre for exploring the central Moor, where the main road from Moretonhampstead to Tavistock and Yelverton crosses the East Dart river. It is first recorded as a name in 1670. The name seems to be derived from the fact that the bridge carried the earliest post-road over the Moor, between Exeter and

South Cornwall via Tavistock. A few yards to the south of this bridge is the largest and most impressive of the clapper bridges in the National Park. This primitive construction of massive granite slabs (one of which is computed to weigh eight tons) was formerly attributed to the pre-Roman inhabitants of the Moor. It is more likely, however, to have been erected in the thirteenth century when the inner Moor was opened up to some extent for tin-working and pastoral farming, and some kind of recognized trackway came into being between the stannary towns of Chagford and Tavistock. A roadway running due south for rather more than a mile leads to Bellever, formerly a typical Dartmoor farm-house (now gone). A Youth Hostel occupies the modern farm buildings. Hut circles and other prehistoric monuments abound in the neighbourhood of Postbridge. So also do the dreary conifer plantations.

PRINCETOWN is a grim little town for the greater part of the year, chiefly notable as the site of the prison (the worst in England) known to the outer world as 'Dartmoor'. This prison was built in 1806 for French and American prisoners taken during the Napoleonic Wars, and there are some remains (including the fine megalithic gateway) of this period; but visitors are understandably discouraged from lingering anywhere near the buildings. The prison was closed when the wars ended in 1815, but was reopened in 1850 as a convict prison and has since been considerably enlarged.

The town itself contains very little of interest, except the ponies which have, unfortunately, learnt to visit the streets and to accept food from visitors. Attractive and innocuous as this pastime appears to be, it is in fact a source of great danger to the animals and motorists alike, as the ponies are encouraged to stray on the roads. Visitors to Dartmoor, and to Princetown in particular, are begged not to feed the animals in this way. The prison is also an attractive sight to some curious minds, but it will be generally agreed that the habit of examining it through field-glasses in the hope of seeing its occupants is not a civilized practice.

The surrounding moorlands have not been improved by the erection of the television mast and building on North Hessary Tor.

SAMPFORD SPINEY is a remote spot on the high ground above the Walkham valley. The 'village centre' of church and Hall Farm is boulder-strewn and picturesque. Easton Town is another good moorland farmhouse, and so is Woodtown, near Walkham. The oakwoods of the Walkham valley are still some of the most beautiful in Devon.

SHEEPSTOR takes its name from the distinctive tor to the north-east of the small village. Much of the parish is high moorland, thickly dotted with Bronze Age antiquities (of which details will be found in the archaeological gazetteer). Ringmoor Down, Ditsworthy Warren, and Yellowmead Down are especially notable in this respect. Indeed, the upper Plym valley is one of the richest parts of Dartmoor for prehistoric remains. The parish church is a pleasant little building, rebuilt in early Tudor times and entirely in granite. In the churchyard is buried Rajah Brooke of Sarawak, who bought an estate at Burrator in 1858 and died here ten years later. His nephew, who succeeded him as Rajah, is also buried here.

The Burrator reservoir is the largest and the most beautiful in Devon. It was constructed in 1891-98 for the Plymouth Corporation, and was enlarged to 150 acres in 1928. It now has a capacity of 1,026 million gallons. The wooded banks, with the broken background of tors, make it perhaps the most beautiful artificial lake in England, far superior to the lake in Blenheim Park which is often accorded that distinction.

SOUTH BRENT is a large village and was formerly a market-town. Important fairs are still held here on the last Tuesday in April and September, mainly for the sale of sheep and cattle. On the high moors are many remains of the Bronze Age inhabitants of the Moor—hut circles, enclosures, and barrows. From Brent Hill (1,019 feet) there are immense views over the South Hams, one of the richest parts of Devon. The parish church is especially interesting to students of architectural history, for the Norman tower (now at the west end) was formerly the central tower of a cruciform church of which the western half has now been destroyed. The Norman font of red sandstone is a fine example of a local type.

SOUTH ZEAL is a village on the old Exeter–Okehampton road, and was formerly a borough. The Oxenham Arms, a good early sixteenth-century granite building, was formerly a house of the Burgoyne family. Oxenham, now a house dated 1714, was the seat of the Oxenhams from the time of Henry III until 1814. West Week is dated 1656 and was the seat of another moorland family—the Battishills. North Week or Wyke, a house of fifteenth- and seventeenth-century date, has been considerably restored (at times regardless of expense) and has lost much of its original character. Wickington, which retains more of its original atmosphere, is largely a fifteenth-century house with a tower-porch.

At South Tawton, the parish church is a handsome fifteenth-century building with carved bosses in the roof and a fine monument to John Wyke of North Wyke (1592). The Church House (*c.* 1500) near by is one of the best examples of its kind in Devon. Above South Zeal rises the huge rounded shoulder of Cosdon (called Cawsand Beacon on the map), from the summit of which one gets impressive views of the Moor to the south and of cultivated farmlands to the north.

THROWLEIGH is one of the most satisfying villages and parishes within the National Park. The parish church is decidedly 'atmospheric'. Structurally it is mostly a granite building of the late fifteenth century, with a dignified west tower. Notice also the admirable priest's doorway, the pulpit made up from pieces of the late medieval screen, and the east window with glass by Sir Ninian Comper.

Part of the attractiveness of the church is derived from its setting at the village centre, which is one of the most pleasing in Devon. Among the interesting buildings in this group are the Old Parsonage (eighteenth century), the Early Tudor Church House, and the Barton. The lower-lying part of the parish is a tangle of deep lanes joining a number of good moorland farmhouses. Of these the most notable are Clannaborough, Shilstone, North Wonson, and Wonson Manor. On the uplands of the parish, which rise to over 1,500 feet, are many hut circles and other remains of the Bronze Age. The White Moor stone circle is one of the best monuments of its kind on Dartmoor, with a diameter of 66 feet, but is little known. The scenery in the parish, on both high ground and low, is everywhere delightful.

TWO BRIDGES is a small cluster of houses where the old road from Chagford to Tavistock crossed the West Dart. The earliest reference to a bridge here occurs in the fifteenth century. The old bridge has now been by-passed by a concrete structure. Two Bridges is an important road-junction where the two main roads over the Moor cross each other. About half a mile up the road towards Moretonhampstead is Crockern Tor, on the summit of which the so-called Tinners' Parliament met at irregular intervals and enacted the special laws that governed the stan-naries (Latin *stannum* = tin). The so-called Judge's Chair on the summit was shifted long ago to Dunnabridge Pound on the Ashburton road. Crockern Tor has never been associated with Druidical sacrifices as is so often stated; the more quickly the visitor to Dartmoor forgets all about the Druids the better. Farther along the Moreton road, and a little off it, lie the ruined Powder Mills, which will interest students of early industrial buildings. Near by is a good example of a clapper bridge over the Cherry Brook. The remarkable piece of primeval woodland known as Wistman's Wood (see the chapter on the Natural History of the Moor) lies about two miles up the valley of the West Dart from Two Bridges (Plate 5). On the opposite hillside runs the Devonport Leat, cut in

1793–96 to supply the growing dockyard town of Devonport (then called Dock) with water and winding away for miles along the contours. It is taken off the West Dart a short distance above Wistman's Wood.

WALKHAMPTON village lies at the south-western end of a vast parish which runs far up on to the Moor and is strewn with prehistoric antiquities of all kinds—hut circles, stone rows and circles, cairns and pounds. There are also tinners' smelting-houses or blowing-houses in the upper Meavy valley, but the 2½-inch map is usually necessary to discover their exact location. Much of the picturesque Yelverton and Princetown railway ran through the parish. The Walkham valley from Merrivale down to Huckworthy Bridge is wooded and very attractive for walkers. The river name means 'the rolling one' and aptly describes the nature of the stream for the greater part of its course.

WARREN HOUSE INN takes its name from one of the extensive warrens or game preserves of which there were several on medieval Dartmoor, in this instance Headland Warren which lay on the hill-slopes to the east. The inn, which replaces an older house that formerly stood on the opposite side of the road, stands alone about 1,400 feet above sea level and is a welcome sight in any season of the year. A footpath leads down to the headstream of the West Webburn and the remains of the Vitifer tin-mine, where the artificial ravines created by the old tin-workers before the days of shaft-mining are among the most striking of their kind (Plate 13), and provide nesting-sites for a small colony of ring ouzels. Some of the best whortleberries may be found along the edges of these scars.

The surrounding moor is thickly marked with 'antiquities' of various periods and should be explored on foot with the aid of the 2½-inch maps. Bennett's Cross, a mile along the road towards Moretonhampstead, was an early guide-post on the wild track from Chagford to Tavistock, and also formed one of the boundary posts of the Headland Warren. It is of medieval date, possibly thirteenth century (Plate 18).

WIDECOMBE IN THE MOOR is probably the best known of all the Dartmoor villages and is by far the most commercialized. In its natural state it was typical of the true moorland villages, but the intelligent visitor will not wish to linger in it today. The so-called Widecombe Fair is of no great antiquity and is quite alien to the nature and spirit of Dartmoor. All the roads leading to it are best avoided around that date (the second Tuesday in September). The village lies in the broad valley of the East Webburn river and takes its name from the wide combe. The parish church is well worth visiting. Often called 'the cathedral of the moor', it is a fourteenth-century cruciform church, reconstructed and enlarged in the late fifteenth century (Plate 20). The western tower of granite is one of the noblest in the west of England and is traditionally supposed (probably correctly) to have been built at the expense of the local tinners in the early sixteenth century when the trade was enjoying a boom. There is much to interest the visitor inside. Outside, the Church House is a fine example of its kind (built about 1500), and now belongs to the National Trust. The Glebe House, also a sixteenth-century building, forms part of the attractive group at the village centre.

The by-roads of the parish are strikingly attractive, and link together a great number of typical moorland farmhouses. Of these the best are Uphill and Sweaton at Ponsworthy, Lake at Poundsgate, Bonehill, Bittleford, Foxworthy, Liswell, Great Dunstone, Venton, Chittleford, Cockingford Mill, Southcombe, Uppacott, and Lower Tor (Plates 16, 17). Ollsbrim or Ouldsbroom, about 1½ miles east of Dartmeet, is particularly interesting as one of the few surviving examples of the ancient 'long house' plan, still in use and almost unchanged. A house is first recorded here in 1317, but the present building is probably about 1600 in date. Corndon Ford, about one mile due north over the Moor, is a fine example of an unchanged Dartmoor yeoman's farmhouse, still being farmed in real Dartmoor fashion. The porch is dated 1718 but the house is generally much older. The student of English vernacular building will find Widecombe parish vastly rewarding and will make his own discoveries. At Blackaton, 1½ miles north-west of Widecombe village, a deserted medieval village has recently been found. On Dockwell Farm at a site known as Hutholes, another deserted medieval village has been located and partly excavated. There are ten or possibly twelve house-sites similar to those at Hound Tor (see under Manaton), of which one house has been completely excavated. The granite-walled houses are probably of twelfth- and thirteenth-century date, as at Hound Tor, but underneath them have been found traces of post-holes of earlier wattle and daub houses presumably dating from late Saxon times. There is no doubt that other deserted village sites remain to be discovered in various parts of the Moor. These sites were probably abandoned at the time of the Black Death (1349–50) but a somewhat earlier desertion cannot be entirely ruled out of consideration.

YELVERTON is a sad note to end upon. Although it is an ancient settlement, first recorded as long ago as 1291, it has developed as a dormitory suburb for Plymouth and is a distressing example of semi-urban growth on a delightful site. The historically-minded visitor may, however, see here the Plymouth Leat which was constructed in 1591 to bring water from the Moor down to the growing Elizabethan naval base. It passes immediately south of the church. The Devonport Leat, constructed in 1793–96 to supply the rival dockyard town, runs roughly parallel with the Plymouth Leat to the north of the church. Roborough Down, to the north-west of Yelverton, provides a number of bracing walks and good views.

BIBLIOGRAPHY

EWANS, M. C. *The Haytor Granite Tramway and Stover Canal.* David & Charles. 1966. The full story of this strangest of early railway systems.

HARRIS, HELEN. *The Industrial Archaeology of Dartmoor.* David & Charles. 1968. A well-illustrated survey of the numerous remains of abandoned industry.

Index

Printed in England for Her Majesty's Stationery Office
by The Campfield Press, St. Albans

Dd. 503642 K72 10/72

The Country Code

GUARD AGAINST ALL RISK OF FIRE

Plantations, woodlands and heaths are highly inflammable: every year acres burn because of casually dropped matches, cigarette ends or pipe ash.

FASTEN ALL GATES

even if you found them open. Animals can't be told to stay where they're put. A gate left open invites them to wander, a danger to themselves, to crops and to traffic.

KEEP DOGS UNDER PROPER CONTROL

Farmers have good reason to regard visiting dogs as pests; in the country a civilised town dog can become a savage. Keep your dog on a lead wherever there is livestock about, also on country roads.

KEEP TO THE PATHS ACROSS FARM LAND

Crops can be ruined by people's feet. Remember that grass is a valuable crop too, sometimes the only one on the farm. Flattened corn or hay is very difficult to harvest.

AVOID DAMAGING FENCES, HEDGES AND WALLS

They are expensive items in the farm's economy; repairs are costly and use scarce labour. Keep to recognised routes, using gates and stiles.

LEAVE NO LITTER

All litter is unsightly, and some is dangerous as well. Take litter home for disposal; in the country it costs a lot to collect it.

SAFEGUARD WATER SUPPLIES

Your chosen walk may well cross a catchment area for the water supply of millions. Avoid polluting it in any way. Never interfere with cattle troughs.

PROTECT WILD LIFE, WILD PLANTS AND TREES

Wild life is best observed, not collected. To pick or uproot flowers, carve trees and rocks, or disturb wild animals and birds, destroys other people's pleasure as well.

GO CAREFULLY ON COUNTRY ROADS

Country roads have special dangers: blind corners, high banks and hedges, slow-moving tractors and farm machinery or animals. Motorists should reduce their speed and take extra care; walkers should keep to the right, facing oncoming traffic.

RESPECT THE LIFE OF THE COUNTRYSIDE

Set a good example and try to fit in with the life and work of the countryside. This way good relations are preserved, and those who follow are not regarded as enemies.

THE COUNTRY CODE
An illustrated booklet is obtainable free from
Her Majesty's Stationery Office or through any bookseller

Other illustrated Guides in the National Park Series

Snowdonia	**32½p**	(39p)
Peak District	**45p**	(51½p)
North York Moors	**35p**	(42½p)
Lake District	**42½p**	(50p)
Northumberland	**37½p**	(43p)
Exmoor	**42½p**	(50p)
Brecon Beacons	**50p**	(56½p)
Yorkshire Dales	**45p**	(51½p)

Prices in brackets include postage

Please send your orders or requests for free lists of titles or guide books to Her Majesty's Stationery Office, P6A (ZD) Atlantic House, Holborn Viaduct, London EC1P 1BN

 **HMSO BOOKS**